WOOD-
SONG

WOOD-SONG

BY

GARY PAULSEN

SCHOLASTIC INC.
New York Toronto London Auckland Sydney

ISBN 0-590-45052-2

Text copyright © 1990 by Gary Paulsen. Illustrations copyright © 1990 by Ruth Wright Paulsen. All rights reserved. First published by Bradbury Press, a division of Macmillan Publishing Company. This edition published by Scholastic Inc., 730 Broadway, New York, NY 10003, by arrangement with Viking Penguin, a division of Penguin Books USA Inc.

36 35 34 33 32 31 30 29 28 27 26 25   3/0

40

Printed in the U.S.A.

First Scholastic printing, September 1991

This book is dedicated to Cookie,
who died on September 10, 1989.

"Her soul is on the raven's wing. . . ."

MAP OF THE IDITAROD

RUNNING

I UNDERSTOOD almost nothing about the woods until it was nearly too late. And that is strange because my ignorance was based on knowledge.

Most of my life it seems I've been in the forest or on the sea. Most of my time, sleeping and waking, has been spent outside, in close contact with what we now call the environment, what my uncles used to call, simply, "the woods."

We hunted. Small and large game. We hunted and killed and though I think now that it is wrong to hunt and kill, at the time I did not think this and I spent virtually all my time hunting.

And learned nothing.

Perhaps the greatest paradox about understanding "the woods" is that so many who enjoy it, or seem to enjoy it, spend most of their time trying to kill parts of it.

Yet, it was a hunter, a wild one, and an act of almost

unbelievable violence that led me to try to understand all of it, and to try to learn from it without destroying it.

I lived in innocence for a long time. I believed in the fairy-tale version of the forest until I was close to forty years old.

Gulled by Disney and others, I believed Bambi always got out of the fire. Nothing ever really got hurt. Though I hunted and killed it was always somehow clean and removed from reality. I killed yet thought that every story had a happy ending.

Until a December morning . . .

I was running a dog team around the side of a large lake, just starting out on my trapline. It was early winter and the ice on the lake wasn't thick enough to support the sled and team or I would have gone across the middle. There was a rough trail around the edge of the lake and I was running a fresh eight-dog team so the small loop, which added five or so miles, presented no great difficulty.

It was a grandly beautiful winter morning. The temperature was perhaps ten below, with a bright sun that shone through ice crystals in the air so that everything seemed to sparkle. The dogs were working evenly, the gangline up through the middle of them thrumming with the rhythm it has when they are working in perfect tandem. We skirted the lake, which lay below and to the right. To the left and rising higher were willows and brush, which made something like a wall next to the trail.

The dogs were still running at a lope, though we had come over seven miles, and I was full of them; my life was full of them. We were, as it happens sometimes, dancing with winter. I could not help smiling, just smiling idiotically at the grandness of it. Part of the chant of an ancient Navajo prayer rolled through my mind:

> *Beauty above me*
> *Beauty below me*
> *Beauty before me . . .*

That is how I felt then and frequently still feel when I am running dogs. I was in and of beauty and at that precise moment a doe, a white-tailed deer, exploded out of some willows on the left side of the team, heading down the bank toward the lake.

The snow alongside the trail was about two feet deep and powdery and it followed her in a white shower that covered everything. She literally flew over the lead dog who was a big, white, wolfy-looking male named Dollar. He was so surprised that he dropped, ducked, for part of an instant, then rose—almost like a rock skipping on the trail—and continued running. We were moving so fast and the deer was moving so fast that within a second or two we were several yards past where it had happened and yet everything seemed suspended in slow motion.

Above all, in the deer, was the stink of fear. Even in that split part of a second, it could be smelled. It could be seen. The doe's eyes were so wide they seemed to come out of her head. Her mouth was jacked open and her tongue hung out to the side. Her jaw and neck were covered with spit, and she stunk of fear.

Dogs smell fear at once but I have not always been able to, even when I was afraid. There is something coppery about it, a metallic smell mixed with the smell of urine and feces, when something, when somebody, is afraid. No, not just afraid but ripped with fear, and it was on the doe.

The smell excited the dogs and they began to run faster, although continuing down the trail; I turned to look back from the sled and saw why the doe was frightened.

Wolves.

They bounded over the trail after the doe even as I watched. These were not the large timber wolves but the smaller northern brush wolves, perhaps weighing forty or fifty pounds each, about as large as most of my team. I think they are called northern coyotes.

Except that they act as wolves. They pack and have pack social structures like timber wolves, and hunt in packs like timber wolves.

And they were hunting the doe.

There were seven of them and not one looked down the trail to see me as they jumped across the sled tracks after the deer. They were so intent on her, and the smell of her, that I might as well not have existed.

And they were gaining on her.

4

I stood on the brakes to stop the sled and set the snow-hook to hold the dogs and turned. The dogs immediately swung down off the trail toward the lake, trying to get at the wolves and deer. The snowhook came loose and we began to slide down the lake bank. I jerked the hook from the snow and hooked it on a small poplar and that held us.

The doe, in horror now, and knowing what was coming, left the bank of the lake and bounded out onto the bad ice. Her tail was fully erect, a white flash as she tried to reach out and get speed, but the ice was too thin.

Too thin for all the weight of her on the small, pointed hooves and she went through and down in a huge spray of shattered ice and water.

She was up instantly, clambering and working to get back up on top of the ice next to the hole. Through sheer effort in her panic she made it.

But it slowed her too much.

In those few moments of going through the ice and getting out she lost her lead on the wolves and they were on her.

On her.

In all my time in the woods, in the wondrous dance of it, I have many times seen predators fail. As a matter of fact, they usually fail. I once saw a beaver come out of a hole on the ice near his lodge in the middle of winter and stand off four wolves. He sustained one small bite on his tail and inflicted terrible damage with his teeth on the wolves, killing one and wounding the other three. I have seen rabbits outwit foxes and watched red squirrels tease martens and get away with it, but this time it was not to be.

I had never seen wolves kill a large animal and indeed have not seen it since. It was horrible and I was not prepared for it. I thought I had great knowledge of how everything in the woods worked. I had hunted and trapped and I had been in the army and seen and done some awful things, but I was still not mentally prepared for the killing.

Largely because of Disney and posed "natural" wildlife films and television programs I had preconceived ideas about wolves, about what wolves should be and do. They never really spoke to the killing.

Spoke to the blood.

In films they would go to the edge of it, and then show the carcass being eaten. In books they always seemed to describe it clinically and technically.

And it is neither clinical nor technical.

There is horror in it.

Wolves do not kill "clean." (If there can be such a thing.) It is a slow, ripping, terrible death for the prey and only those who have not seen it will argue for that silly business about the prey actually selecting itself.

Two wolves held the doe by the nose, held her head down to the ice, and the other wolves took turns tearing at her rear end, pulling and jerking and tearing, until they were inside of her, pulling out parts of her and all this time she was still on her feet, still alive.

I did not have a gun or I think I would have used it. I was having some trouble with the dogs as the blood smell excited the wolf in them. They wanted to be at the kill. They were jerking and pulling on the gangline so hard I thought it would break, and I stumbled down in the deep snow along the lake bank and held them—one bit me on the hand—but I could not stop looking.

It was all in silence.

She was still on her feet though they had the guts out of her now, pulled back on the ice, eating and pulling, and I wanted it to end, wanted it to be over for her.

And she sank.

She somehow did not die then and still does not die in my mind. She just sinks. Over and over I can see her sinking as they pull at her. When I could stand it no longer, when I was sick with it and hated all wolves for the horror of it, I yelled.

"Leave her . . ."

And I think I cursed as well but it didn't matter. When I yelled it was as if a film had stopped. The wolves somehow had not known I was there. They had been so intent on killing, on the smell of it, that they had not seen me or the dogs and the sound of my voice stopped them.

But it did not frighten them.

The doe was down now, spread and down and steaming out the rear, and all the wolves stopped dead and turned to look at me and the dogs.

Just that. Look.

And I knew that it was wrong for me to have yelled, that I was interrupting something I did not understand, some ancient thing I did not know any more than I knew what it was like to live in the Ice Age.

They stopped and studied me.

7

One of them, I think a male because he was larger than the others, raised on his hind legs to see better over some low willows in front of me and when he raised—standing like a man—the morning sun caught his head and I could see that it was completely covered in blood.

Steaming with it. He'd been inside her and he was soaked with blood and the snow all around the back of the doe was soaked with blood, a great red apron of blood. He stood for two, three seconds, staring at me and through me, knowing me, and I began to understand some of it then.

I began to understand that they are not wrong or right— they just are.

Wolves don't know they are wolves.

That's a name we have put on them, something we have done. I do not know how wolves think of themselves, nor does anybody, but I did know and still know that it was wrong to think they should be the way I wanted them to be.

And with that thought, with that small understanding, came the desire to learn, to know more not just about wolves but about all things in the woods. All the animals, all the dances . . .

And it started with blood.

· 2 ·

CONSIDERING the enormous effect dogs have had on my life, I came to them late and in an odd-enough way.

I was forty years old and living in poverty when I first became involved with sled dogs. Writing is a strange way to make a living, and I had sold many books by the time I was forty but was not making enough money to live on. I worked construction, ran heavy equipment, tracked satellites, taught—did many things to support life—and by the time I was forty I was working very hard and had become almost completely broke, living with my wife and son in a small cabin in northern Minnesota with no plumbing, no electricity, and no real prospects.

And so to dogs.

The state of Minnesota was having a rough time with beavers. They had more or less run amuck and were damming up rivers and flooding highways, filling pastures, even beginning to invade the cities. I had trapped a bit when I was a boy, and to make some money I decided to trap for the state—the state paid a small bounty and the pelt brought a similar small amount of money.

It was a one-man operation, and not very successful because I ran it on foot—or on a pair of skis when the snow came—and I rarely got over a twenty-mile trapline. (There was also the difficulty that I had trouble even then with trapping and killing; I was not good at it because I did not really want to do it.)

Some friends heard of my trapping and gave me four older dogs—they were Storm, Yogi, Obeah, and Columbia—and a broken sled—the siderails were broken and needed replacement—and so I was into dogs.

But of course I was not. I did not know how to run them, or be run by them. I did not even know how to harness them or hook them properly to the gangline that pulled the sled when they were harnessed.

But I fixed the sled and tried to harness them and that first time I did not know about, well, anything. The dogs more or less wandered around the yard without leaving and I thought it was madness to even try to use them when the only way they would leave the yard was for me to drag them.

After a time I stopped and sat on a stump and watched them and tried to think of a way to make them run. Finally I decided you couldn't make them, you had to let them.

One of the dogs, Obeah, seemed to be trying to look ahead, and I thought he might want to pull the others. Lead them. So I put him in front and it worked. We left the yard and ran on a trail through the woods and I thought all the Yukon King thoughts there are.

I was running a team in the north and they were out there ahead of me and it was beautiful. . . .

And I knew nothing.

I was so ignorant, so steeped in not knowing, that I did not even know what I didn't know. I didn't know what questions to ask, or how to ask them, and I would not begin to learn until Storm taught me.

His blood taught me.

There will be more about running dogs later, and more about Storm, but for the moment it is enough to know that when I started I thought I knew what I was doing. The dogs moved for me. I expanded the trapline to nearly sixty miles over the next three months. By the middle of hard winter I thought I was Sergeant Preston—a Mountie on a radio show I had listened to as a child.

By this time I had three more dogs—a seven-dog work team—and a tent. Obeah had evolved into something I thought was a good leader. I think this was largely because he looked like a sled dog should look—like a Sergeant Preston kind of sled dog. He was large and wolf-like, with a thick gray mane and a tail that curled over his back. He was standoffish. He did not want to be petted. Now and again he would lift his lip at me, and twice he bit me on the leg. Obeah always wanted to fight other males and I thought—mistakenly—that all of this was proper behavior for a sled dog.

At least the Yukon King type of sled dog I had always dreamed about.

I wasn't trapping very much and I was running a long distance—it took three days to run the sixty-mile line. But I confined my running to the daylight. I did not know about using a head lamp, did not know that the dogs ran better at night. I would run during the day, work on my trap sets, then pitch a tent and camp at night and harness up and run the next day, and there was great beauty in that.

Sleeping with them. I would fix the tent and arrange my sleeping bag and pad and then put the dogs around me in a circle just outside the firelight. On truly cold nights, when it dropped to ten or fifteen below, I would bring several of the dogs into the tent and pack them around the bag tightly and fall asleep with them breathing around me, with their hearts beating against me through the bag, with their souls in the tent with me. They also felt the warmth and would move in closer against the bag, jamming into the sides. On one very cold night—it must have been thirty or thirty-five below—I awakened in the morning with dogs all around me and three of them curled up on top of me; a living blanket.

With all this closeness, with all the running, with the dance of the dogs, I thought I knew them and with that thought—with that attitude—I wasn't learning anything.

I just ran the line, took a beaver now and then, and pretended somewhere in my mind that I was Sergeant Preston and had a whole team of Kings out in front of me.

Until Storm taught me.

There came a night, finally, when I was about twenty

12

miles from home and it was very cold—close to forty below—and rather than spend the night out camping, I decided to run in the dark and go on home.

Running sled dogs is much like sailing a boat on the ocean. Distances are almost critically relative. Sailing a hundred miles with the wind might take twelve or fourteen hours, depending on wind strength, boat, and sailor. To turn around and sail the same hundred miles against the wind, and especially if there is a current against you, might take one, even two weeks. Indeed, sometimes it simply can't be done. Ever.

Dogs are much the same. Twenty miles with a work team traveling seven miles an hour—which is about average—would seem to take about three hours. And sometimes does. But an inch of new snow to slow the sled, or an extra heavy load to slow it still more, perhaps a head wind to cap it, and the dogs can only make three or four miles an hour. Suddenly the trip—the same twenty miles—becomes a five-, six-, or even seven-hour run. And on a seven-hour run with a heavy load it is necessary to stop and rest the dogs, let them sleep for a couple of hours and feed them, so that adds still more.

All of these things were against me. A run I thought would take three hours was in reality going to take me closer to nine hours, all in the dark and intense cold, in new snow and what turned out to be hilly country, with a sled that weighed close to five hundred pounds, fully loaded.

It became one of the longest nights of my life.

I did not understand at that time that you should feed the

dogs straight raw meat and fat. It is the same as putting gasoline in an engine. Some people actually told me that meat was bad for them and to only feed them dry dog food. I had a sack of dog food with me and fed that to them when I stopped to camp.

All wrong. All of it wrong. What I did not know then is not only should the dogs be fed meat and fat, but they most decidedly should not be fed dry dog food when they are going to work hard or be stressed at all. The bits of ground corn used as a base for the dog food are worthless and largely indigestible. And they are very sharp. When a working dog's stomach tightens, as it does when he pulls, the corn becomes like tiny little knives that cut and tear at the insides of his intestines. . . .

I knew none of this.

And so to Storm.

Storm was an almost classic sled dog. He looked much like a brindle wolf, with beautifully slanted eyes. He had a great reach to his front legs and a thick mane and straight back. In many ways he was still very primitive, but he liked people a great deal and would lean against your leg to be petted.

He pulled.

Of course they all pull. It is genetic, so old a code or command that it has become part of what sled dogs are; the fiber of their very being. When they are six months old you harness them and they pull. There is no training necessary. It just is.

But some of them pull better than others. Storm pulled from somewhere within himself, from some primitive core so strong that he could not not pull, even if he wanted to.

He was also what is known as an "honest" dog. Some dogs pull and when they get tired they slack off but they keep enough pull on the harness tug so it appears they are working while they are really resting. When they have rested for a quarter mile or so they go back to work. It's not bad; it's very much one of those they-know-you-know-they-know situations and part of running dogs. But some dogs, and Storm was one of them, pull hard all the time, even when they are tired. These are called "honest" dogs and are keyed to running somehow more than other dogs.

So into this night, in my ignorance, we started to run; into what I thought would be a three- or four-hour easy run we started.

And it was not so bad at first.

Part of it showed me new beauty. There was a full moon and when we first started the night run we went across a lake, a beautiful, long lake, in the moonlight. The moonlight off the snow in the cold air was so bright and flat white you could have read a book, and the dogs worked wonderfully in the cold. At the end of the lake there was a large hill. The base of the hill was heavily forested and the trail wound through the trees.

As the dogs moved through the dark shadows of the forest and climbed the hill we went through some strange kind of temperature inversion, and just as they came back out into the moonlight, into the flat-white light at the top of the hill, the steam from their collective breath came up and over their backs and hid them.

When dogs run they are silent. Only in the movies do they rattle and bark while they are running. So in silence, all in silence except for the gentle whuffing of their breath and the slight jingle of their harness snaps, I was pulled over the top of the open hill in the moonlight by a steam ghost.

It was heart-stoppingly beautiful.

And that was part of that run.

We ran down from the hill through some country that a tornado had ripped and torn. For six or seven miles the trail wound through the wreckage of downed trees and broken limbs.

It was hard going, with the new snow, and frequently having to stop and chop through downed trees with an axe, then hump the sled over them; hacking and swearing and pushing, the dogs slamming and jerking and pulling until finally we got through and were in calm forest again, winding through thick spruce trees. In and out of dappled moonlight and beauty. The sweat was freezing on the outside of my clothes as it steamed out so I had to stop and scrape it off with a stick and suddenly, for no reason that I knew, Storm sprayed blood.

In the moonlight I could not tell that it was blood, but only something dark that sprayed out of his rear end. Storm was directly in front of the sled in the wheel position (a term that dates back to stagecoaches) and it covered the front end of the sled and the sides of the trail; a sudden dark liquid.

I stopped the sled and tied it off to a tree. I thought he had developed diarrhea—which was bad enough—and I ran up to his side.

He stood normally, slamming into the harness to get the sled moving. The temperature had dropped still more and the dogs all wanted to run. They work to the cold—the colder the better.

The smell was wrong.

As I kneeled next to him near the stain in the snow, the smell was wrong for what I thought it was. I lit a match and was horrified to see blood.

Storm was spraying bright red blood out his rear end. Blood covered the sled and the trail. I had never, never seen this, known this before; had never hurt a dog before.

And now this.

All the dogs were screaming—high-pitched deafening screams because they were impatient and wanted to run, knowing they were heading in the direction of home.

Storm ignored me and kept screaming and lunging to go as if nothing were wrong.

And each time he lunged blood squirted.

I became frantic. In my life blood meant something bad; something fiercely bad. Blood was an end. I didn't know what to do. I stood next to him and did not know what to do.

Doctor, I thought—I need to get him to a doctor before he dies. And without any more pulling. I had to ease him down and get him to a doctor. That's all I could think.

I unhooked him from the gangline and carried him, lunging and screaming, to the sled. I tied him in the basket of the sled with a short piece of line to his collar. Then I stood on the runners and let the team loose.

We didn't make fifty yards before Storm went absolutely insane. When he looked ahead in the darkness and saw that other dogs were pulling while he was riding on the sled he went mad. He flopped and ripped and tore at the sled, at the rope holding him by the collar, at me—at the world— until he had worked himself off to the side of the sled and was pulling there, pulling with the rope on his collar, pulling so his neck was warped back around.

I stopped and put him back on the sled and tried to start again but it was no good. He immediately fought to get down again, screamed for it, and when he got down he began to pull with his neck.

I tried a longer rope, tried to let him trot along in back, and that did not work either. He simply ran up alongside until the rope caught, then began to pull, his neck wrapped around to the side.

They do not really know harness. When Captain Cook first saw Eskimos and their dogs in Alaska they did not have harnesses. The dogs pulled from crude collars. Storm didn't care that he wasn't hooked in a harness. The collar would do fine.

He pulled the way they have always pulled.

And there it was. I could not stop because I thought if I waited too long to get him to a doctor he would bleed to death. I could not get him to ride the sled because if I did the exertion of his slamming around trying to get back out and pull made him bleed all the more. I could not get him to trot easily along in back.

Finally, in a kind of mad worry, I took off his harness and

let him run free, thinking he might just follow us as we made our way through the darkness.

Instead he immediately ran up and around the sled and into his old position. He tried to pull even though he wasn't hooked to anything. And I thought for a moment that might work—at least he didn't have the weight of the sled to pull. But he bled anyway, and seemed to work hard anyway, and seemed to be pulling hard anyway. Because he wasn't hooked to anything, whenever there was some unevenness in the trail he would lunge ahead and trip and nearly fall. When he stumbled, the sled almost ran over him—which almost certainly would have killed him. At last I knew that I could do nothing but what he wanted to do.

Let him pull.

It was a terrible thing to learn on that night because of his blood. Blood was so important to me, meant so much to me, and here it was, leaving him and I thought his life was leaving him. Finally done, I put the harness back on him and hooked him up and made the run through the night thinking that I was allowing him to die.

Seven more hours we ran. I stopped along the way to snack the dogs on dry food and bits of meat. They ate the snow. And Storm pulled.

Across two rivers and several lakes and through some sharp hills in the moonlight we ran and Storm pulled and I waited for him to end, hating myself for doing the only thing I thought I could do.

But it was nothing to him.

To Storm it was all as nothing. The blood, the anxiety I

felt, the horror of it meant as little to Storm as the blood from the deer on the snow had meant to the wolves. It was part of his life and if he could obey the one drive, the drive to be in the team and pull, then nothing else mattered.

And he did not die. Later, when he was very old, Storm would teach me about death, but not that night. That night he ran and we ran until just before dawn I could see the glow from the Coleman lamp coming through the windows of the cabin across the swamp near our home. He never once faltered, and did not falter for six more years, never stopped pulling. I took the dogs out of harness and rubbed their shoulders and marveled at Storm, who stood with his tail wagging, not bleeding any longer. I put them on their chains so they could get at the fresh straw in their houses to make soft beds and realized that I had learned something again that night. I had learned that I knew absolutely nothing— the same lesson I learned from the wolves and the doe— knew nothing about animals, understood nothing about the drives that make them work, knew nothing.

And I also learned—as with the wolves and the doe—that I wanted to know more, wanted to know everything there was to know about dogs and the woods and running with a team.

But I had one more important lesson to learn first, and it would also be in blood.

·**3**·

COLD can be very strange. Not the cold felt running from the house to the bus or the car to the store; not the chill in the air on a fall morning, but deep cold.

Serious cold.

Forty, fifty, even sixty below zero—actual temperature, not windchill—seems to change everything. Steel becomes brittle and breaks, shatters; breath taken straight into the throat will freeze the lining and burst blood vessels; eyes exposed too long will freeze; fingers and toes freeze, turn black, and break off. These are all known, normal parts of intense cold.

But it changes beauty as well. Things are steeped in a new clarity, a clear focus. Sound seems to ring and the very air seems to be filled with diamonds when ice crystals form.

On a river in Alaska while training I once saw a place where a whirlpool had frozen into a cone, open at the bottom like a beautiful trap waiting to suck the whole team down. When I stopped to look at it, with the water roaring through at the bottom, the dogs became nervous and stared down into the center as if mystified and were very glad when we moved on.

After a time I stopped trapping. That change—as with many changes—occurred because of the dogs. As mentioned, I had hunted when I was young, trapping and killing many animals. I never thought it wrong until the dogs came. And then it was a simple thing, almost a silly thing, that caused the change.

Columbia had a sense of humor and I saw it.

In the summer the dogs live in the kennel area, each dog with his own house, on a chain that allows him to move in a circle. They can only run with the wheeled carts on cool nights, and sometimes they get bored being tied up. To alleviate the boredom we give the dogs large beef bones to chew and play with. They get a new bone every other day or so. These bones are the center of much contention—we call them Bone Wars. Sometimes dogs clear across the kennel will hold their bones up in the air, look at each other, raise their hair, and start growling at each other, posturing and bragging about their bones.

But not Columbia.

Usually Columbia just chewed on his bone until the meat was gone. Then he buried it and waited for the next bone. I never saw him fight or get involved in Bone Wars and I always thought him a simple—perhaps a better word would be primitive—dog, basic and very wolf-like, until one day when I was sitting in the kennel.

I had a notebook and I was sitting on the side of Cookie's roof, writing—the dogs are good company for working—when I happened to notice Columbia doing something strange.

He was sitting quietly on the outside edge of his circle, at the maximum length of his chain. With one paw he was pushing his bone—which still had a small bit of meat on it—out and away from him, toward the next circle.

Next to Columbia was a dog named Olaf. While Columbia was relatively passive, Olaf was very aggressive. Olaf always wanted to fight and he spent much time arguing over bones, females, the weather—anything and everything that caught his fancy. He was much scarred from fighting, with notched ears and lines on his muzzle, but he was a very good dog—strong and honest—and we liked him.

Being next to Columbia, Olaf had tried many times to get him to argue or bluster but Columbia always ignored him.

Until this morning.

Carefully, slowly, Columbia pushed the bone toward Olaf's circle.

And of all the things that Olaf was—tough, strong, honest—he wasn't smart. As they say, some are smarter than others, and some are still not so smart, and then there was Olaf. It wouldn't be fair to call Olaf dumb—dogs don't measure those things like people—but even in the dog world he would not be known as a whip. Kind of a big bully who was also a bit of a doofus.

When he saw Columbia pushing the bone toward him, he began to reach for it. Straining against his chain, turning and trying to get farther and farther, he reached as far as he could with the middle toe on his right front foot, the claw going out as far as possible.

But not quite far enough. Columbia had measured it to the millimeter. He slowly pushed the bone until it was so close that Olaf's claw—with Olaf straining so hard his eyes bulged—just barely touched it.

Columbia sat back and watched Olaf straining and pushing and fighting and when this had gone on for a long time—many minutes—and Olaf was still straining for all he was worth, Columbia leaned back and laughed.

"Heh, heh, heh . . ."

Then Columbia walked away.

And I could not kill or trap any longer.

It happened almost that fast. I had seen dogs with compassion for each other and their young, and with anger and joy and hate and love but this humor went into me more than the other things.

It was so complicated.

To make the joke up in his mind, the joke with the bone and the bully, and then set out to do it, carefully and quietly, to do it, then laugh and walk away—all of it was so complicated, so complex, that it triggered a chain reaction in my mind.

If Columbia could do that, I thought, if a dog could do that, then a wolf could do that. If a wolf could do that, then a deer could do that. If a deer could do that, then a beaver, and a squirrel, and a bird, and, and, and . . .

And I quit trapping then.

It was wrong for me to kill.

But I had this problem. I had gone over some kind of line with the dogs, gone back into some primitive state of exaltation that I wanted to study. I wanted to run them and learn from them. But it seemed to be wasteful (the word *immature* also comes to mind) to just run them. I thought I had to have a trapline to justify running the dogs, so I kept the line.

But I did not trap. I ran the country, and camped and learned from the dogs and studied where I would have trapped if I were going to trap. I took many imaginary beaver and muskrat but I did no more sets and killed no more animals. I will not kill anymore.

Yet the line existed. Somehow in my mind—and until writing this I have never told another person about this—the line still existed and when I had "trapped" in one area I would extend the line to "trap" in another, as is proper when you actually trap. Somehow the phony trapping gave me a purpose for running the dogs, and would until I began to train them for the Iditarod, a dogsled race across Alaska, which I had read about in *Alaska* magazine.

But it was on one of these "trapping" runs that I got my third lesson, or awakening.

There was a point where an old logging trail went through a small, sharp-sided gully—a tiny canyon. The trail came down one wall of the gully—a drop of fifty or so feet—then scooted across a frozen stream and up the other side. It might have been a game trail that was slightly widened, or an old foot trail that had not caved in. Whatever it was, I came onto it in the middle of January. The dogs were very excited. New trails always get them tuned up and they were fairly smoking as we came to the edge of the gully.

I did not know it was there and had been letting them run, not riding the sled brake to slow them, and we virtually shot off the edge.

The dogs stayed on the trail but I immediately lost all control and went flying out into space with the sled. As I did, I kicked sideways and caught my knee on a sharp snag, felt the wood enter under the kneecap and tear it loose.

I may have screamed then.

The dogs ran out on the ice of the stream but I fell onto it. As these things often seem to happen, the disaster snowballed.

The trail crossed the stream directly at the top of a small, frozen waterfall with about a twenty-foot drop. Later I saw the beauty of it, the falling lobes of blue ice that had grown as the water froze and refroze, layering on itself. . . .

But at the time I saw nothing. I hit the ice of the stream bed like dropped meat, bounced once, then slithered over the edge of the waterfall and dropped another twenty feet onto the frozen pond below, landing on the torn and separated kneecap.

I have been injured several times running dogs—cracked ribs, a broken left leg, a broken left wrist, various parts frozen or cut or bitten while trying to stop fights—but nothing ever felt like landing on that knee.

I don't think I passed out so much as my brain simply exploded.

Again, I'm relatively certain I must have screamed or grunted, and then I wasn't aware of much for two, perhaps three minutes as I squirmed around trying to regain some part of my mind.

When things settled down to something I could control, I opened my eyes and saw that my snow pants and the jeans beneath were ripped in a jagged line for about a foot. Blood was welling out of the tear, soaking the cloth and the ice underneath the wound.

Shock and pain came in waves and I had to close my eyes several times. All of this was in minutes that seemed like hours and I realized that I was in serious trouble. Contrary to popular belief, dog teams generally do not stop and wait for a musher who falls off. They keep going, often for many miles.

Lying there on the ice I knew I could not walk. I didn't think I could stand without some kind of crutch, but I knew I couldn't walk. I was a good twenty miles from home, at least eight or nine miles from any kind of farm or dwelling.

It may as well have been ten thousand miles.

There was some self-pity creeping in, and not a little chagrin at being stupid enough to just let them run when I didn't know the country. I was trying to skootch myself up to the bank of the gully to get into a more comfortable position when I heard a sound over my head.

I looked up and there was Obeah looking over the top of the waterfall, down at me.

I couldn't at first believe it.

He whined a couple of times, moved back and forth as if he might be going to drag the team over the edge, then disappeared from view. I heard some more whining and growling, then a scrabbling sound, and was amazed to see that he had taken the team back up the side of the gully and dragged them past the waterfall to get on the gully wall just over me.

They were in a horrible tangle but he dragged them along the top until he was well below the waterfall, where he scrambled down the bank with the team almost literally falling on him. They dragged the sled up the frozen stream bed to where I was lying.

On the scramble down the bank Obeah had taken them through a thick stand of cockleburs. Great clumps of burrs wadded between their ears and down their backs.

He pulled them up to me, concern in his eyes and making a soft whine, and I reached into his ruff and pulled his head down and hugged him and was never so happy to see anybody probably in my life. Then I felt something and looked down to see one of the other dogs—named Duberry—licking the wound in my leg.

She was not licking with the excitement that prey blood would cause, but with the gentle licking that she would use when cleaning a pup, a wound lick.

I brushed her head away, fearing infection, but she persisted. After a moment I lay back and let her clean it, still holding onto Obeah's ruff, holding onto a friend.

And later I dragged myself around and untangled them and unloaded part of the sled and crawled in and tied my leg down. We made it home that way, with me sitting in the sled: and later when my leg was sewed up and healing and I was sitting in my cabin with the leg propped up on pillows by the wood stove; later when all the pain was gone and I had all the time I needed to think of it . . . later I thought of the dogs.

How they came back to help me, perhaps to save me. I knew that somewhere in the dogs, in their humor and the way they thought, they had great, old knowledge; they had something we had lost.

And the dogs could teach me.

· 4 ·

THE adventure really begins in differences—the great differences between people and animals, between the way we live now and the way we once lived, between the Mall and the Woods.

Primarily the difference between people and animals is that people use fire. People create fire, and animals don't. Oh, there are minor things—like cars and planes and all the other inventions we seem to have come up with. But in a wild state, the real difference is that we use controlled fire.

And it was in the business of fire that I came to the first of many amazements inside the woods.

It started with a campfire.

I was on a hundred-mile run in deep winter with new dogs—pups, really, just over a year old. I had gone beyond the trapping stage and was training new dogs for a possible attempt on the Iditarod. The pups had lived in kennels, mostly. They had only been on short training runs so that almost everything they saw on this run was new to them. They had to learn to understand as they ran.

A cow in a field was a marvel and had to be investigated; it took me half an hour to get untangled from the fence. A ruffed grouse that flew down the trail ahead of us had to be chased. A red squirrel took the whole team off the trail into the woods, piling into deep drifts and leaving us all upside down and packed with snow.

It was, in short, a day full of wonders for them and when night came and it was time to stop—you can really only do about twenty miles a day with young dogs—we found a soft little clearing in the spruce trees. I made beds for them and when they were fed and settled, or as settled as young dogs can get, I made a fire hole in the snow in the center of the clearing, next to the sled, and started a small fire with some dead popple. It was not a cold night so the fire was very small, just enough to melt some snow and make tea. The flames didn't get over a foot high—but the effect was immediate and dramatic.

The dogs went crazy with fear. They lunged against their chains, slamming and screaming. I went to them and petted them and soothed them and at length they accepted the fire. I put their frozen blocks of meat around the edges of the flames to soften, and fed them warm meat. Then they sat and stared at the flames, the whole ring of them.

Of course they had never seen fire, or flame, in the kennel—it was all completely new to them. But the mystery was why they would automatically fear it. They had seen many new things that day, and they didn't fear anything but the fire.

And when they were over the fear of it, they were fascinated with it. I stretched my foam pad and sleeping bag out in the sled to settle in for the night. This is a complicated process. The felt liners for my shoepacs had to be taken off and put down inside the bag so my body heat could dry them for the next day. My parka had to be turned inside out so all the sweat from the day could freeze and be scraped off in the morning. Any wet clothing had to be flattened and worked down into the bag to dry as well. While I was doing all this in the light from my head lamp, I let the fire die down.

Just as I started to slide into the bag one of the dogs started to sing. It was the sad song.

They have many songs and I don't know them all. There is a happy song they sing when the moon is full on the snow and they are fed and there is a rain song, which is melancholy—they don't like rain very much—and there is a song they sing when you have been with them in the kennel and start to walk away, a come-back-and-don't-go-away sad song.

That was the song one dog had started to sing. When I turned to look at him he was staring where the fire had died down into a cup in the snow, and in a moment the rest of them had picked up the song and were wailing and moaning for the lost fire, all staring where the flames had been.

In an hour they had gone from some coded, genetic fear of fire, to understanding fire, to missing it when it went away.

"Cave people must have gone through this same process. I wondered how long it had taken us to understand and know fire. The pups had done it in an hour and I thought as I pulled the mummy bag up over my head and went to sleep how smart they were or perhaps how smart we weren't and thought we were.

⤙⤙⤙⤙⤙⤙

$ometimes when they run it is not believable. And even when the run is done and obviously happened it is still not believable.

On a run once when it was the perfect temperature for running, twenty below—cold enough for the dogs to run cool, but not so bitterly cold as to freeze anything exposed—I thought I would just let them go and see what they wanted to do. I wouldn't say a word, wouldn't do anything but stand on the back of the sled—unless a bootie or a quick snack was needed. I'd let them run at an easy lope. I thought I would let them go until they wanted to stop and then only run that way from then on, and they ran to some primitive instinct, coursed and ran for seventeen hours without letup.

One hundred and seventy-five miles.

And they didn't pant, weren't tired, could have done it again. I nearly froze—just a piece of meat on the back of the sled—but they ran and ran in a kind of glory and even now I can't quite believe it.

The second incident with fire was much the same—something from another world, another time. It happened, but is not quite believable.

We had run long in a day—a hundred and fifty miles—with an adult team in good shape. The terrain had been rough, with many moguls (mounds of snow) that made the sled bounce in the trail. I had taken a beating all day and I was whipped. I made beds and fed the dogs and built up a large fire. It had been a classic run but I was ready for sleep. It was nearly thirty below when I crawled into the sleeping bag.

I was just going to sleep, with my eyes heavy and the warmth from the fire in my face, when the dogs started an incredible uproar.

I opened my eyes and there was a deer standing right across the fire from me.

A doe. Fairly large—more than a year old—standing rigid, staring at me straight on in the face across the fire. She was absolutely petrified with terror.

At first I thought she had somehow stupidly blundered into the camp and run past the dogs to the fire.

But she hung there, staring at me, her ears rotating with the noise of the dogs around her. She did not run and still did not run and I thought she must be a medicine doe sent to me; a spirit doe come in a dream to tell me something.

Then I saw the others.

Out, perhaps thirty yards or more beyond the camp area, but close enough for the fire to shine in their eyes—the others. The wolves. There was a pack of brush wolves and they had been chasing her. I couldn't tell the number, maybe five or six; they kept moving in agitation and it was hard to pin them down, but they were clearly reluctant to let her go, although they were also clearly afraid of me and being close to me. Unlike timber wolves, brush wolves are not endangered, not protected, and are trapped heavily. We are most definitely the enemy, and they worried at seeing me.

And when I saw them I looked back at the doe and could see that she was blown. Her mouth hung open and spit smeared down both sides with some blood in it. They must have been close to getting her when she ran to the camp.

And the fire.

She must have smelled her death to make the decision she made. To run through the circle of dogs, toward the fire and the man was a mad gamble—a gamble that I wasn't a deer hunter, that the dogs weren't loose or they would have been on her like the wolves, that somehow it would be better here.

All those choices to make at a dead, frantic run with wolves pulling at her.

This time it had worked.

I sat up, half raised, afraid to move fast lest she panic and run back into the wolves. I had more wood next to the sled and I slowly put a couple of pieces on the fire and leaned back again. The wolves were very nervous now and they moved away when I put the wood on the fire, but the doe stayed nearby for a long time, so long that some of the dogs actually went back to lying down and sleeping.

She didn't relax. Her body was locked in fear and ready to fly at the slightest wrong move, but she stayed and watched me, watched the fire until the wolves were well gone and her sides were no longer heaving with hard breathing. She kept her eye on me, her ears on the dogs. Her nostrils flared as she smelled me and the fire and when she was ready—perhaps in half an hour but it seemed like much more—she wheeled, flashed her white tail at me, and disappeared.

The dogs exploded into noise again when she ran away, then we settled back to watching the fire until sleep took us. I would have thought it all a dream except that her tracks and the tracks of the wolves were there in the morning.

Fear comes in many forms but perhaps the worst scare is the one that isn't anticipated; the one that isn't really known about until it's there. A sudden fear. The unexpected.

And again, fire played a role in it.

We have bear trouble. Because we feed processed meat to the dogs there is always the smell of meat over the kennel. In the summer it can be a bit high because the dogs like to "save" their food sometimes for a day or two or four—burying it to dig up later. We live on the edge of wilderness and consequently the meat smell brings any number of visitors from the woods.

Skunks abound, and foxes and coyotes and wolves and weasels—all predators. We once had an eagle live over the kennel for more than a week, scavenging from the dogs, and a crazy group of ravens has pretty much taken over the puppy pen. Ravens are protected by the state and they seem to know it. When I walk toward the puppy pen with the buckets of meat it's a toss-up to see who gets it—the pups or the birds. They have actually pecked the puppies away from the food pans until they have gone through and taken what they want.

Spring, when the bears come, is the worst. They have been in hibernation through the winter, and they are hungry beyond caution. The meat smell draws them like flies, and we frequently have two or three around the kennel at the same time. Typically they do not bother us much—although my wife had a bear chase her from the garden to the house one morning—but they do bother the dogs.

They are so big and strong that the dogs fear them, and the bears trade on this fear to get their food. It's common to see them scare a dog into his house and take his food. Twice we have had dogs killed by rough bear swats that broke their necks—and the bears took their food.

We have evolved an uneasy peace with them but there is the problem of familiarity. The first time you see a bear in the kennel it is a novelty, but when the same ones are there day after day, you wind up naming some of them (old Notch-Ear, Billy-Jo, etc.) There gets to be a too relaxed attitude. We started to treat them like pets.

A major mistake.

There was a large male around the kennel for a week or so. He had a white streak across his head which I guessed was a wound scar from some hunter—bear hunting is allowed here. He wasn't all that bad so we didn't mind him.

He would frighten the dogs and take their hidden stashes now and then, but he didn't harm them and we became accustomed to him hanging around. We called him Scarhead and now and again we would joke about him as if he were one of the yard animals.

At this time we had three cats, forty-two dogs, fifteen or twenty chickens, eight ducks, nineteen large white geese, a few banty hens—one called Hawk which will come up again later in the book—ten fryers which we'd raised from chicks and couldn't (as my wife put it) "snuff and eat," and six woods-wise goats.

The bears, strangely, didn't bother any of the yard animals. There must have been a rule, or some order to the way they lived because they would hit the kennel and steal from the dogs but leave the chickens and goats and other yard stock completely alone—although you would have had a hard time convincing the goats of this fact. The goats spent a great deal of time with their back hair up, whuffing and blowing snot at the bears—and at the dogs who would *gladly* have eaten them. The goats never really believed in the truce.

There is not a dump or landfill to take our trash to and so we separate it—organic, inorganic—and deal with it ourselves. We burn the paper in a screened enclosure and it is fairly efficient, but it's impossible to get all the food particles off wrapping paper, so when it's burned the food particles burn with it.

And give off a burnt food smell.

And nothing draws bears like burning food. It must be that they have learned to understand human dumps—where they spend a great deal of time foraging. And they learn amazingly fast. In Alaska, for instance, the bears already know that the sound of a moose hunter's gun means there will be a fresh gut pile when the hunter cleans the moose. They come at a run when they hear the shot. It's often a close race to see if the hunter will get to the moose before the bears take it away. . . .

Because we're on the south edge of the wilderness area we try to wait until there is a northerly breeze before we burn so the food smell will carry south, but it doesn't always help. Sometimes bears, wolves, and other predators are already south, working the sheep farms down where it is more settled—they take a terrible toll of sheep—and we catch them on the way back through.

That's what happened one July morning.

Scarhead had been gone for two or three days and the breeze was right, so I went to burn the trash. I fired it off and went back into the house for a moment—not more than two minutes. When I came back out Scarhead was in the burn area. His tracks (directly through the tomatoes in the garden) showed he'd come from the south.

He was having a grand time. The fire didn't bother him. He was trying to reach a paw in around the edges of flame to get at whatever smelled so good. He had torn things apart quite a bit—ripped one side off the burn enclosure—and I was having a bad day and it made me mad.

I was standing across the burning fire from and without thinking—because I was so used to —I picked up a stick, threw it at him, and yelled, "Get out of here."

I have made many mistakes in my life, and will probably make many more, but I hope never to throw a stick at a bear again.

In one rolling motion—the muscles seemed to move within the skin so fast that I couldn't take half a breath—he turned and came for me. Close. I could smell his breath and see the red around the sides of his eyes. Close on me he stopped and raised on his back legs and hung over me, his forelegs and paws hanging down, weaving back and forth gently as he took his time and decided whether or not to tear my head off.

I could not move, would not have time to react. I knew I had nothing to say about it. One blow would break my neck. Whether I lived or died depended on him, on his thinking, on his ideas about me—whether I was worth the bother or not.

I did not think then.

Looking back on it I don't remember having one coherent thought when it was happening. All I knew was terrible menace. His eyes looked very small as he studied me. He looked down on me for what seemed hours. I did not move, did not breathe, did not think or do anything.

And he lowered.

Perhaps I was not worth the trouble. He lowered slowly and turned back to the trash and I walked backward halfway to the house and then ran—anger growing now—and took the rifle from the gun rack by the door and came back out.

He was still there, rummaging through the trash. I worked the bolt and fed a cartridge in and aimed at the place where you kill bears and began to squeeze. In raw anger, I began to take up the four pounds of pull necessary to send death into him.

And stopped.

Kill him for what?

That thought crept in.

Kill him for what?

For not killing me? For letting me know it is wrong to throw sticks at four-hundred-pound bears? For not hurting me, for not killing me, I should kill him? I lowered the rifle and ejected the shell and put the gun away. I hope Scarhead is still alive. For what he taught me, I hope he lives long and is very happy because I learned then—looking up at him while he made up his mind whether or not to end me—that when it is all boiled down I am nothing more and nothing less than any other animal in the woods.

·**5**·

WE burn wood to heat the house and we have a wood-burning, old-time kitchen stove. There is probably nothing that makes me feel quite as warm as coming in on a cold winter morning, leaning over the kitchen stove to warm my hands, and smelling rich pine woodsmoke and fresh bread baking in the oven.

The cats love the wood stove, too. They spend most of the winter either pressed against the side of it or sleeping beneath it. We had a neighbor—an old bachelor—who let the chickens into his house. They would roost on the stove each night to stay warm as the fire died down. It made an unholy mess—chickens cannot be housebroken—and when he fired the stove up and it cooked the chicken stuff the smell would drive you out, but he seemed to like it and the chickens provided company for him.

We don't let the animals in, except for house dogs (we have three loose little terrier kind of things) and, of course, the cats, but the chickens have discovered that the chimney conducts heat as well as smoke out of the house. It's usual in the winter to go out in the morning and see chickens on the roof, flocked around the chimney warming themselves. (They have a perfectly good, insulated coop but we let them run because it makes the eggs taste better, and they prefer the chimney to the coop.)

One of them is a banty hen we call Hawk, and since she is at least partially a creature of the woods it might be proper to tell about her here.

Banties—my wife says—are mean, small chickens you can never get rid of. They can indeed be mean, but they are wonderfully self-sufficient and fun to have around even if it takes about thirty of their small eggs to make a decent omelet. They are forever setting on nests hatching out chicks, brooding and clucking and attacking anything that comes close. Mother love takes on whole new meaning when you cross a banty hen taking care of fifteen or twenty chicks. I have seen grown men run when they get attacked by this small chicken.

I was running a team in the late spring—we pull a wheeled cart with a platform on the back (rather like a sled with wheels) when there is no snow. We were on a county road near thick forest when we came on a dead ruffed grouse. She probably got hit by a car while gathering gravel for her gizzard; grouse come out to the road each evening and get stones to help grind up the seeds and berries they eat and are frequently hit by cars. The dogs had her in an instant before I could stop them and she was gone—feathers floating in the air. As we started on our way, I happened to glance into the low brush and saw her nest. I tied the dogs off so they wouldn't run—again, I had some pups in the team and they were insane, especially after finding the grouse—and I went to the nest.

There were fourteen eggs cuddled in the soft grass and leaves. They looked so forlorn that I picked them up and carried them in my cap rather than leaving them for some passing skunk. I'm not sure what I expected to do with them. My wife is an artist and I thought perhaps she might want them for a still life, but when I got home with the dogs—the eggs somehow unbroken, cradled in my pack bouncing on the rig—I saw Hawk sitting on her clutch of eggs.

So I popped the grouse eggs under her—she pecked my hand bloody for the effort—just to see what would happen.

My wife later said that I unleashed a summer of terror on us when I put the eggs under Hawk.

The eggs hatched out. Every single grouse egg, along with her own ten eggs, hatched out and she adopted them. The baby grouse—and there isn't anything cuter than a grouse chick—bonded with Hawk and thought she was their mother.

Within days of hatching she had the whole brood coursing the yard looking for bugs or bits of grain that we threw to them. If they saw a grasshopper the whole mob would take after it.

Hawk was a protective mother and the chicks, both grouse and chicken, grew fast and well.

That's when things got out of hand.

The grouse chicks didn't know they were supposed to be chickens. Except for short distances banty chickens can't fly well, because they have been bred to be too heavy for their wings. But the grouse rapidly grew into adolescents with good wing feathers. They were soon flying all over the yard—whipping from tree to tree or up to the roof.

Hawk would watch them and call to them and at first they came, gathering under her wings for protection—even when they were so large they would lift her up off the ground when they all piled under her.

When the grouse chicks grew enough to ignore Hawk, it made her furious to lose control. The young grouse flew away from her up into the trees even when she ordered them to come to her, and her anger made her fluff up and stomp around. She took it out on all of us.

Next to the house was the woodpile. It was as high as the roof of the house—we use wood for cooking and heating so it becomes a major pile—and Hawk took to sitting on top of the woodpile, watching the yard and her chicks to protect them no matter how far they ranged.

Nothing dared move in the yard.

The first time I noticed it was when Russel—our fat old tom cat—was goobering around in the yard. He made the mistake of crouching and pretending to stalk one of the chicks. The frightened chick made one small distress peep and that's all it took.

I was standing in the driveway facing the woodpile and saw Hawk launch herself like a speckled red missile. She hit Russel in the back of the head so hard cat hair flew out in a circle. Then she hung on and rode him out of the yard, raking his sides like a professional bull rider.

That first attack opened the door for her and she began to rule the yard with an iron hand from the top of the woodpile. She watched like a hawk (hence her name) and woe unto anybody or anything that stepped too close to her chicks. Since as the chicks grew they scattered all over the place, and since there were over twenty of them, it was impossible to not be near one of her chicks. The yard became a war zone.

Images:

My wife carrying laundry to the line and going to her knees as Hawk catches her in the back of the head; Hawk flying off to the right clutching a pair of shorts in her claws.

Quincy, our smallest terrier, keeping a low profile as he tries to sneak across the yard and get to the relative safety of the lilacs near the driveway; Quincy flopping end over end as Hawk nails him in the back of the head like a feathered cannonball.

My son—six-foot-two—coming back from the mailbox with an armload of mail, getting smashed full in the face just as he steps over the battery-powered electric fence we use to keep the goats out of the yard; paper and envelopes flying through the air as his legs hit the wires.

Fred, our obese half-lab yard dog, crouching down with all his hair up and very many teeth showing, facing Hawk who has her neck feathers ruffled out and her beak down as they get ready for head-to-head battle. Hawk winning.

A fox drawn by the meat smell from the kennel but pulled into the yard by the chicks; the fox grabbing a chick and getting hit so hard by Hawk coming from the top of the woodpile that I could see spit fly as the chick was blown out of his mouth.

And finally, my wife coming into the house; tomatoes she'd been carrying from the garden crushed all over her shirt, her hair a mess around the bicycle helmet she'd started to wear for protection around the yard, and anger in her eye.

"The Hawk," she said, grabbing a towel and wiping herself off, "strikes again."

The grouse grew up and most of them went back to the wild. As they left, Hawk mellowed.

But the people and animals who lived through the episode still tiptoe across the yard when Hawk is sitting on the woodpile.

·6·

MYSTERIES.

Sometimes things happen in the woods that are not supposed to happen, mysterious things that make the hair go up on your neck, unexplainable, out-of-place things.

I was sitting by a brush pile one fall morning—we'd been hunting mushrooms and I had the team and small cart tied up some distance away—when a chipmunk came out on a log at the base of the brush pile and chukkered at me. Chipmunks are very tame, and it's common to have them eat out of your hand. I was eating a cookie so I leaned forward and held it out and the chipmunk would come toward me a couple of inches, then go back, then forward and back, getting closer to the cookie piece in my fingers all the time. Suddenly a red squirrel—not much larger than the chipmunk—jumped down from the top of the brush pile, ran out on the log, and attacked the chipmunk.

For a part of a second I thought she was fighting for the right to get the cookie, but I was wrong. In half a moment she turned the chipmunk over, grabbed him by the throat, killed him, then dragged the chipmunk back down the length of the log to a shadowed place at the edge of the brush pile and began to eat him.

It was so fast, so brutal, that I hadn't had time to move, and it was completely without reason. Red squirrels are not carnivorous—they eat the insides of pine cones. They most decidedly do not attack and eat chipmunks. Ever.

I wanted it not to be. I wanted the cute little chipmunk to still be sitting on the log coming for the piece of cookie in my hand, wanted the red squirrel to be sitting on a limb holding a pine nut in her hand, turning it and nibbling.

Not sitting back in the shadows pulling the guts out of a chipmunk.

I have never seen it before or since. One moment of stark, staggering violence for no reason, with no sense—there and gone—but I will always be able to see the squirrel looking at me over her kill, nose and front chisel teeth and muzzle dripping blood.

There are night ghosts.

Some people say that we can understand all things if we can know them, but there came a dark night in the fall when I thought that was wrong, and so did the dogs.

We had been running all morning and were tired; some

of the dogs were young and could not sustain a long run. So we stopped in the middle of the afternoon when they seemed to want to rest. I made a fire, set up a gentle, peaceful camp, and went to sleep for four hours.

It hadn't snowed yet so we had been running with a three-wheel cart, which meant we had to run on logging roads and open areas. I had been hard pressed to find new country to run in to keep the young dogs from becoming bored and this logging trail was one we hadn't run. It had been rough going, with a lot of ruts and mud and the cart was a mess so I spent some time fixing it after I awakened, carving off the dried mud. The end result was we didn't get going again until close to one in the morning. This did not pose a problem except that as soon as I hooked the dogs up and got them lined out—I was running an eight-dog team— my head lamp went out. I replaced the bulb and tried a new battery, but that didn't help—the internal wiring was bad. I thought briefly of sleeping again until daylight but the dogs were slamming into the harnesses, screaming to run, so I shrugged and jumped on the rig and untied it. Certainly, I thought, running without a head lamp would not be the worst thing I had ever done.

Immediately we blew into the darkness and the ride was madness. Without a lamp I could not tell when the rig was going to hit a rut or a puddle. It was cloudy and fairly warm—close to fifty—and had rained the night before. Without the moon or even starlight I had no idea where the puddles were until they splashed me—largely in the face— so I was soon dripping wet. Coupled with that, tree limbs

I couldn't see hit at me as we passed, almost tearing me off the back of the rig. Inside an hour I wasn't sure if I was up, down, or sideways.

And the dogs stopped.

They weren't tired, not even a little, judging by the way they had been ripping through the night, but they stopped dead.

I had just taken a limb in the face and was temporarily blinded. All I knew was that they had stopped suddenly and that I had to jam down on the brakes to keep from running over them. It took me a couple of seconds to clear my eyes and when I did, I saw the light.

In the first seconds I thought it was another person coming toward me. The light had an eerie green-yellow glow. It was quite bright and filled a whole part of the dark night ahead, down the trail. It seemed to be moving. I was in deep woods and couldn't think what a person would be doing there—there are no other teams where I train—but I was glad to see the light.

At first.

Then I realized the light was strange. It glowed and ebbed and seemed to fill too much space to be a regular light source. It was low to the ground, and wide.

I was still not frightened, and would probably not have become frightened except that the dogs suddenly started to sing.

I have already talked about some of their songs. Rain songs and first-snow songs and meat songs and come-back-and-stay-with-us songs and even puppy-training songs, but I had heard this song only once, when an old dog had died in the kennel. It was a death song.

And that frightened me.

They all sat. I could see them quite well in the glow from the light—the soft glow, the green glow, the ghost glow. It crept into my thinking without my knowing it: the ghost glow. Against my wishes I started thinking of all the things in my life that had scared me.

Ghosts and goblins and dark nights and snakes under the bed and sounds I didn't know and bodies I had found and graveyards under covered pale moons and death, death, death . . .

And they sang and sang. The cold song in the strange light. For a time I could do nothing but stand on the back of the wheeled rig and stare at the light with old, dusty terror.

But curiosity was stronger. My legs moved without my wanting them to move and my body followed them, alongside the team in the dark, holding to each dog like a security blanket until I reached the next one, moving closer to the light until I was at the front and there were no more dogs to hold.

The light had gotten brighter, seemed to pulse and flood back and forth, but I still could not see the source. I took another step, then another, trying to look around the corner, deeply feeling the distance from the dogs, the aloneness.

Two more steps, then one more, leaning to see around the corner and at last I saw it and when I did it was worse.

It was a form. Not human. A large, standing form glowing

in the dark. The light came from within it, a cold-glowing green light with yellow edges that diffused the shape, making it change and grow as I watched.

I felt my heart slam up into my throat.

I couldn't move. I stared at the upright form and was sure it was a ghost, a being from the dead sent for me. I could not move and might not have ever moved except that the dogs had followed me, pulling the rig quietly until they were around my legs, peering ahead, and I looked down at them and had to laugh.

They were caught in the green light, curved around my legs staring at the standing form, ears cocked and heads turned sideways while they studied it. I took another short step forward and they all followed me, then another, and they stayed with me until we were right next to the form.

It was a stump.

A six-foot-tall, old rotten stump with the bark knocked off, glowing in the dark with a bright green glow. Impossible. I stood there with the dogs around my legs, smelling the stump and touching it with their noses. I found out later that it glowed because it had sucked phosphorus from the ground up into the wood and held the light from day all night.

But that was later. There in the night I did not know this. Touching the stump, and feeling the cold light, I could not quite get rid of the fear until a black-and-white dog named Fonzie came up, smelled the stump, snorted, and peed on it.

So much for ghosts.

In new snow there can be no secrets, no mysteries. Everything leaves tracks. It is possible to see where the owl took the mouse when it tried to run across the snow in the night; the perfect pattern of the owl's wing feathers hitting the powder-snow as the bird dropped on the mouse is there.

You can see the intricate necklace-pattern of tracks made by a hunting ermine as it looks for mice, going down into the under-snow cities the mice have in the swamp grass during the winter, then exploding out the top again with the kill, and down again for another one.

The tracks are always there, and they always tell the truth.

But once I came on a clearing about forty feet across. Dead in the middle of the clearing a fox had taken a grouse. On cold winter nights and days grouse make small caves in the snow to keep from freezing and if they are caught in the caves they can be taken. It is easy to find the holes they make when they plummet into the snow but very hard to catch them off guard because when they hear the sound of someone or something coming through the snow, they explode up and out in a white cloud.

But a fox had taken one in its cave and eaten it. The feathers were there. The tracks of the kill were there.

But there were no tracks leading out to the center of the clearing, no fox tracks around the grouse cave. Nothing. No tracks leaving, no tracks coming.

I tied the dogs off to a tree and took the snowshoes from

the sled and spent the better part of an hour trying to work it out, moving around in the new snow. There were no fox tracks anywhere in the neighborhood. I moved out in larger and larger circles and could find no fox tracks, no sign that a fox had come from anywhere or gone anywhere. The more I looked the less I could find. There could not have been a fox, simply could not have been one and yet there was.

Somehow.

One fox. One grouse. In the middle of the clearing and nowhere else on earth. A quick death, a handful of feathers, then nothing.

Cedar waxwings—small cardinal-like birds that are largely gray—come in the first part of spring. You'd think that over the thousands, perhaps millions, of years they have been migrating they would have worked it out to arrive in the north country at the right time, but they always come early, while there is still snow and no real food for them.

When we see them coming in small flocks, we put out suet for them. They hit the kennels and steal meat but they would rather have berries and seeds.

High-bush cranberries taste—according to my grand-mother—like somebody's old socks. Perhaps they aren't that bad, but they do smell awful when they're cooked and it takes a lot of sugar to make high-bush cranberry jelly worth eating. Maybe because of the way they taste the berries are rarely eaten by game early in the fall when they come ripe.

They freeze and hang, beautifully red and luscious-looking, for the whole winter—the color truly is wonderful against the snow. The grouse start to eat them as the winter wears on and they care less about the taste.

The berries are still there in the spring, still frozen, and I happened to be sitting near a high-bush cranberry stand when a flock of cedar waxwings arrived one spring afternoon and that is where I saw another mystery that haunts me.

I had always thought of birds as not terribly intelligent—although Hawk did much to change my mind. I never thought of them as counting, or paying much attention to each other.

But the cedar waxwings didn't just descend on the tree willy-nilly. There was great order as they settled in rows on limbs, eight or ten birds in each row. Then the bird closest to the berries in each row would take a berry carefully and hold it out to the bird next to him in his beak. That bird would take the berry and turn and pass it on to the next, who would take it and turn and give it to the next, and so on until the bird at the end got the berry.

Then the first bird would take another berry and pass it on, and so on, until each bird in the line was holding a berry. When each bird was holding a berry they all faced front and ate them, working the pulp off until they had the meat and spitting out the center pit.

Then they would start over. My wife says it's because they hate the taste of the berries and pass them on hoping to get a sweeter one, and of course there aren't any—they're all sour.

But she's just guessing and I still do not know why they do it.

The doe was something that I could not believe, even when I saw it. . . .

It happened on a night run. It had been cold, but not deep cold—between twenty and thirty below at night—and very still. I was thinking of summer because my feet were cold. My toes have been frostbitten and they get cold easily. Thinking of summer, or Jamaica, or the inside of a red stove helps.

I was thinking specifically of two summer incidents involving deer—one indescribably sweet and the other funny in a painful way.

Both times, I had been fishing in a canoe. There is something about canoes; they do not cause fear. It is possible to paddle gently up to many wild animals and they simply stand and watch—this same thing happens often with dog teams. The silence is probably the cause, but there is grace to a canoe—or a dog team, or a sailboat (which whales allow close to them)—a gentle elegance that seems to fit much more into nature than the roar of an outboard or snowmobile. (Perhaps for that reason in many states it is illegal to hunt from a canoe—deemed unfair—and the same law should apply to dog teams.)

One early summer we had friends visiting us from the city. I took the man and his four-year-old son out in the canoe to work some crappie beds. This morning the crappies were best in close to shore and we caught seven or eight good ones by hanging right on the edge of the lily pads and casting out to the deeper side. The water was very shallow where the canoe floated—not over a foot deep—and the man and I were busy fishing while the young boy, who couldn't cast yet, was having more fun hanging a lure over the shallow side and watching the dozens of small sunfish come to it and nibble.

It was so still the water looked plated with the sky, and absolutely quiet except for a loon that let go once in a while before diving with the high, keening wail and whoop that is so wonderfully soft and melancholy. I was just working my lure in close to the boat when I heard the boy giggle quietly, and I turned to see him reaching out to touch a fawn.

She was new, maybe two, three weeks old, still red with the camouflage spots. She walked out into the water slowly, one careful step at a time, and stretched her nose to touch the finger the boy was holding out, as if they were old friends. It was very deliberate, a youngster meeting another youngster, and I was afraid to breathe lest the moment be broken. I looked up quickly to signal the father but he was seeing it already—his eyes were shining with it—and the moment hung in silence, a moment so incredible in all the moments there are that it seemed magic, staged.

When they had touched, the fawn turned and walked slowly back up into the hazel brush, where I could now see the mother, frantic with worry, trying to get her baby to come back, and then it was done.

Silence, for a long time. Even the small boy was silent.

Finally I coughed. "It's all part of Disneyland of the North," I said. "The fawn comes out on a rail and you touch it and it goes back. . . ."

But it was not a time for jokes and I let it fall. We just sat for a time, watching the hazel brush where the fawn and mother had disappeared, and I had one long, intense moment of gratitude that is still going on, gratitude that I have seen such a thing.

The second time I was canoeing down a flat, winding river that cuts through the woods like a sluggish snake. I had gear in the canoe for a week and I was trying to catch a muskie so I could let it go. (I do not understand why I was doing this either—I have never caught a muskie so I could let it go, though I have tried for several thousand casts, and have to a large degree stopped trying to catch a muskie so I can let it go. It seemed almost a vision quest for a time but it's fading now as I get older and the muskie I didn't catch gets bigger while the muskie I did catch—none—gets smaller.)

It was an incredibly hot day. A late August sun seemed to boil the river and the deerflies and horseflies were not to be believed. I have never seen them worse—it must have been a peak in their cycle. They formed a thick cloud around the canoe so that at times it was impossible to even see the bank. They all bit hard and the blood-smell from the bites brought more of them. They drank repellent like Kool-Aid, licked it off and took more. I tried lighting a smudge in a tin can in the middle of the canoe as I paddled—which worked for mosquitoes—but it didn't bother the flies at all.

They just kept eating and soon my exposed arms and face and hands were bloody.

By accident I discovered a partial solution. The canoe slipped into the shade, under some overhanging cedars, and as if by design some of the flies moved away, back out into the sun to fly along and wait for me to come out again.

In this manner I moved down the river, grabbing shade close in when I could. I was sliding under a leaning cedar when suddenly there was a tremendous crashing sound to my right. I hardly had time to turn when a doe launched herself from the thick brush on the bank in a magnificent arc that carried her out and up, higher than my head, to crash into the shallow water near the bank.

Even in the split second of the event I could see the flies. They were horrendous—a thick mass of them on her head, a swarm trailing back like a comet's tail as she flew through the air. Flies packed into her ears, into her eyes. Flies to drive her mad, insane, temporarily blind.

She had no idea I was there. She landed so close she drenched me with water but in her mad run she'd left the bank blind, wanting only to get in the water and away from the maddening flies.

She jammed her head underwater and slammed it viciously back and forth in a swirling motion then raised it. She snapped it out of the water and was looking straight into my eyes from a distance of four or five feet.

Everything—breath, heart, everything—was absolutely still. Even the flies seemed to stop.

I have never seen such anger, such defiance compressed in a single moment. The flies had taken her beyond control and when she saw me her eyes opened wide in surprise, then seemed to narrow in cold rage. She didn't care that I was man—the enemy—didn't care that I was there, that she was only an arm's reach away. She didn't care about anything right then except the flies. Her eyes, her manner, all things about her for that moment seemed to say: Mess with me and you're a dead man.

Raw, irritated, frustrated, ripping anger.

I didn't move and in that very short time she realized what I was, blew out of the water in a fountain of spray and bottom mud, and was gone.

I thought of her now on the cold night, remembered the wonderfully hot sun cooking down on my back as I paddled. Even the flies seemed to be from the warmth somehow. Musing, lost in the scene, I did not notice that the dogs were slowing and had stopped until my stomach rammed into the handlebar of the sled.

"Pick it up," I said, which usually snapped them into motion, but this time they didn't move. The leader whined in unease and the two wheel dogs—the dogs pulling directly in front of the sled—turned and tried to climb back onto the sled. With their motion several of the other dogs began to growl and I felt the nervousness come back from the dogs and into me.

They'd acted this way before, usually when they'd run into a moose in the dark. We had been attacked by moose on a few occasions and it was not something I wished to do again. Moose are large, and essentially insane with an almost pathological hatred of the dogs, the sled, the musher, trees, trains, cars, and everything else as near as I can figure. When they come at you it's like getting run over by a Buick with legs.

I wished I was some other place.

The nervousness of the team increased and I knew I would have to deal with it, so I set the snowhook and walked up alongside the dogs, flashing my head lamp ahead, trying to see around the slight curve to the lead dog.

He was stopped in the middle of the trail with all his hair up, his lips bared, growling low in his throat.

Ahead of him, slightly to the side of the trail, stood a doe.

She was absolutely still, looking straight ahead over the dog.

None of this made sense. Number one, a deer would not stand so still that close—four, five feet—to a dog. Number two, the dog would not normally have hesitated. He would have been on the deer, or tried to get at her, and all the other dogs would join in. You never moved so fast on a run as when a deer jumped out in front of the team and bolted down the trail. They fairly flew trying to catch it.

And here all of them were whimpering and cowering, spooked by one doe.

Who was standing absolutely still.

And I was getting spooked by her.

She stood staring across the dogs as if they weren't there.

I pushed the dogs sideways on the trail and made my way slowly to the front, closer to the deer.

There weren't three feet between her and the lead dog, who was still whining.

And still she did not move.

Finally I stood so close I could touch her. The light from my head lamp hit her eyes. They were fogged, fogged with death; I could see that she was dead. Standing dead in the night wind next to the trail, guarding the winter night.

She had frozen solid, on her feet, exactly as if she were alive—perfectly still and upright. It could not be yet was; I looked for many things in my mind to explain it. A sudden heart attack, freak paralysis . . . I tried to think of all the possibilities but it still did not make sense and we could not stay.

I could not bring myself to go closer to her, and when I pulled the leader forward and lined him out on the trail and pulled the hook, the team shot past the dead doe without looking up, staring at the ground, not barking or lunging to get at her but moving as fast as possible.

Moving away from that place.

· **7** ·

WE have had and been owned by many dogs since we started to run them. We borrowed many initially because we did not have dogs and they came and went, ran for us awhile, then belonged to someone else. They were loved while they were with us and missed when they left, whatever the reason. Indeed, at the time of this writing we have forty-one dogs, counting the joyful madness we call the puppy pen, and each dog has taught us much.

There is this dog named Fred who has lived with us for going on nine years. When he first came to live with us he made several sled dogs pregnant and so we had him altered. He is loose and moves freely through the kennel, stealing food as he goes. The upshot is that between the operation and the uncontrolled eating Fred has become enormously fat. His weight-for-size should be about forty pounds—and that would be a shade heavy.

Fred came to weigh over a hundred and thirty pounds. He was so heavy his legs sometimes collapsed under him, so we put him on a diet and that is when I began to see and understand temper in dogs.

It was not easy to place restrictions on Fred. He was smarter than us. As soon as we started the extreme weight-loss regimen, Fred began showing up with bits and pieces of food he'd buried all around the yard and kennel over the past year. We took that away, and began taking the food the sled dogs had buried as well, because Fred was stealing from them. Fred still had more—food that he had hidden in the barn—and when we took even that away he began to steal tomatoes and potatoes from the garden. Finally, when we fenced the garden and forced him to go on two-mile walks by dragging him on a leash, Fred began to lose weight.

At the same time he lost his temper. Always a well-minded dog, he stopped coming when we called. He quit his normal watchdog duties—he'd always been a good barker if somebody drove up—and took to sitting in the yard, staring at the house.

Then he bit me.

Fred had never been one to bite although he could be very single-minded in his thinking. One unforgettable incident with the electric fence illustrates his persistence. When we first put the wire in, it was just high enough to catch his tail, which he carried curled up. In due course he clipped the wire and the jolt put him down. In a flash of rage and with a mighty, bellering growl Fred turned on the wire and bit it. And was promptly knocked off his feet. Again—before I could stop him—he bit the wire and again he was knocked down. On the third try he backed off and thought about it. I figured he was done, until he sat up and hit the wire running. Once more it hammered him, but his momentum carried the day and he broke the wire.

Whereupon he stood, wet on it, and walked away growling. (Indeed, he still growls at the wire when he walks by.) He sticks to a thing, but he isn't vicious.

Yet he bit me.

He studied the house, figured I was the reason for his discomfort, waited until I was walking across the yard, and lifted my kneecap as deftly as a surgeon.

It put me on my hands and knees and he moved off a few feet and sat, watching me, panting quietly.

I got the message and we fed him—small amounts, still almost starvation, but something—and Fred returned to his former cheerful self. Although I limped past him cautiously for several months, he never popped me again, but I learned to watch the dogs for signs of irritability and temper.

Different dogs of course have different tempers. Some are more short-tempered than others, but on one occasion I had a whole team mad at me.

It made for a wild ride.

The thing is, it started gently enough. My leader was a sweet dog named Cookie and I had six dogs, all cheerful. It was on the trapline. I had checked several sets and the weather had turned sour. By late afternoon there was a full storm blowing snow so hard it was impossible to see where we were going.

The dogs always know direction but this was before I learned to trust them—learned to understand that lead dogs know more than the person on the sled. Afraid I would get lost in the storm, I challenged every decision. If Cookie wanted to go left, I wanted to go right, if she wanted to go right, I wanted to go left or straight ahead.

Each time she persisted, overriding my commands, I scolded her for fighting me, and each time I would find later that she was right.

Still I did not learn and I continued to challenge them, often causing the team to get tangled. In time they grew sick of my idiocy. When I went up to pull them over, floundering in the deep snow, they ignored me, tried to shrug away my hand. Still trying to be partially polite, they let me know I was being a *putz*, and still I persisted.

Finally I went too far.

We were running along the top edge of a long ridge, higher and higher. The wind was tearing at us. I had my head buried in my parka hood and couldn't even see the front end of the team.

But I was sure I knew the ridge, knew where we were, felt that I had been there before.

I was absolutely, dead wrong.

The team went slower and slower until they were walking, lugging up the middle of the ridge and—perhaps after a quarter of a mile—they stopped. I yelled at them to turn right ("Gee" is the command for right, "Haw" for left). I knew where we were now—was sure of it—but Cookie tried to turn them left, down a long, shallow incline.

I became furious at their mutiny, swore, yelled at the team, then stomped forward, grabbed Cookie by the back of her harness and half-pulled, half-threw her off to the right.

She vanished in the driving snow and wind, moving angrily in the direction I had thrown her. The team followed her, and I jumped on the sled as it went by.

For one or two seconds it was all right. I stood on the brake and held the sled back and we slithered down the hill.

Then it all blew apart. With a great lurch I felt the sled fly out into empty space and drop beneath me. I barely had time to fall backward and go into a tuck before I hit the side of a nearly vertical incline and began to tumble.

I flapped and rolled for what seemed like hours, end over end. I heard the dogs falling beneath me, the sled rolling over and over, and all the gear and food being tossed out, crashing around me.

With a resounding thump the whole pile—sled, dogs, gear, and me, upside down—plummeted into a heap in the bottom of what seemed to be a deep gully.

It was impossible for a moment to understand what had happened. There was not a place where I ended and the dogs and junk began. One dog—named Lad—had his nose jammed squarely in my mouth, another was in my armpit. The sled was on top of me, and if you'd asked me my name I couldn't have told you.

Cookie had knowingly taken the team over the edge of a sharp drop. It was something she never would have done on her own, but I had pushed and griped and hollered too much and she thought it time to give me a lesson.

If I wanted to be stupid, if I persisted in being stupid, if I just couldn't resist being stupid, then she figured I had it coming and she wouldn't hold me back.

It was a good lesson.

But it wasn't over yet. I stood and shook the snow out of my clothes—it was actually packed in my ears—and tipped the sled upright. It took me fifteen minutes to find all the gear and repack the sled and the dogs watched me quietly the whole time.

When the sled was loaded I set to work on the dogs. They were an unholy mess, tangled so badly the gangline was in knots.

The dogs were . . . strange. While I worked to untangle them, it was almost as if I weren't there, as if a robot were working on them. They were pleasant enough, but they did not make eye contact with me. They looked straight ahead while I untangled them. They almost, but not quite, ignored me. Even the dogs that would normally be jumping all over me held back.

It was eerie, quiet even with the wind blowing over the top of the gully. But after a moment I dismissed it as all in my head and went back to the sled.

I pulled the snowhook and stood on the runners.

And the whole team lay down.

They did not drop instantly. But each and every dog, as if by a silent command from Cookie, dug a bit and made a bed and lay down in the snow and went to sleep. I tried every way I knew to get them to run. Fed them, begged them, bit their ears, but they completely ignored me. I wasn't even there.

They didn't get up for eighteen hours.

I had gone over the line.

In the storm, in the pushing and yelling and driving, I had passed the point where they would accept me, run for me, pull for me, and they told me there in that gully. In that wild place they told me so that I would understand that they were the team, they were all of it, and if I ignored them or treated them wrong I would know it.

Finally I pulled out my sleeping bag and made a camp of sorts and heated some tea and dozed and drank tea and thought of how it is to be stupid.

And later, when they felt I'd had enough—late the next day while I was still in the sleeping bag—Cookie stood and shook the snow off. The rest of the dogs did the same, shook and marked the snow. I got out of the bag and fed them and packed and stood on the sled and they pulled up and out of the gully like a runaway train. They pulled up and into the sun and loped all the way home in great joy and glee; joy they were happy to share with me.

Unless I grew stupid again.

It is always possible to learn from dogs and in fact the longer I'm with them the more I understand how little I know. But there was one dog who taught me the most. Just one dog.

Storm.

First dog.

He has already been spoken of once here when he taught

me about heart and the will to pull. But there was more to him, so much more that he in truth could take a whole book.

Joy, loyalty, toughness, peacefulness—all of these were part of Storm. Lessons about life and, finally, lessons about death came from him.

He had a bear's ears. He was brindle colored and built like a truck, and his ears were rounded when we got him so that they looked like bear cub ears. They gave him a comical look when he was young that somehow hung onto him even when he grew old. He had a sense of humor to match his ears, and when he grew truly old he somehow resembled George Burns.

At peak, he was a mighty dog. He pulled like a machine. Until we retired him and used him only for training puppies, until we let him loose to enjoy his age, he pulled, his back over in the power curve so that nothing could stop the sled.

In his fourth or fifth year as a puller he started doing tricks. First he would play jokes on the dog pulling next to him. On long runs he would become bored and when we least expected it he would reach across the gangline and snort wind into the ear of the dog next to him. I ran him with many different dogs and he did it to all of them— chuckling when the dog jumped and shook his or her head— but I never saw a single dog get mad at him for it. Oh, there was once a dog named Fonzie who nearly took his head off, but Fonzie wasn't really mad at him so much as surprised. Fonzie once nailed me through the wrist for waking him up too suddenly when he was sleeping. I'd reached down and touched him before whispering his name.

Small jokes. Gentle jokes, Storm played. He took to hiding things from me. At first I couldn't understand where things were going. I would put a bootie down while working on a dog and it would disappear. I lost a small ladle I used for watering each dog, a cloth glove liner I took off while working on a dog's feet, a roll of tape, and finally, a hat.

He was so clever.

When I lost the hat it was a hot day and I had taken the hat off while I worked on a dog's harness. The dog was just ahead of Storm and when I kneeled to work on the harness—he'd chewed almost through the side of it while running—I put the hat down on the snow near Storm.

Or thought I had. When I had changed the dog's harness I turned and the hat was gone. I looked around, moved the dogs, looked under them, then shrugged. At first I was sure I'd put the hat down, then, when I couldn't find it, I became less sure and at last I thought perhaps I had left it at home or dropped it somewhere on the run.

Storm sat quietly, looking ahead down the trail, not showing anything at all.

I went back to the sled, reached down to disengage the hook and when I did, the dogs exploded forward. I was not quite on the sled when they took off so I was knocked slightly off balance. I leaned over to the right to regain myself, and when I did I accidentally dragged the hook through the snow.

And pulled up my hat.

It had been buried off to the side of the trail in the snow, buried neatly with the snow smoothed over the top so that it was completely hidden. Had the snowhook not scraped down four or five inches I never would have found it.

I stopped the sled and set the hook once more. While knocking the snow out of the hat and putting it back on my head I studied where it had happened.

Right next to Storm.

He had taken the hat, quickly dug a hole, buried the hat and smoothed the snow over it, then gone back to sitting, staring ahead, looking completely innocent.

When I stopped the sled and picked up the hat he looked back, saw me put the hat on my head, and—I swear—smiled. Then he shook his head once and went back to work, pulling.

Along with the jokes, Storm had scale eyes. He watched as the sled was loaded, carefully calculated the weight of each item, and let his disapproval be known if it went too far.

One winter a friend gave us a parlor stove with nickel trim. It was not an enormous stove, but it had some weight to it and some bulk. This friend lived twelve miles away—twelve miles over two fair hills followed by about eight miles on an old, abandoned railroad grade. We needed the stove badly (our old barrel stove had started to burn through) so I took off with the team to pick it up. I left early in the morning because I wanted to get back that same day. It had snowed four or five inches, so the dogs would have to break trail. By the time we had done the hills and the railroad grade, pushing in new snow all the time, they were ready for a rest. I ran them the last two miles to where the stove was and unhooked their tugs so they could rest while I had coffee.

We stopped for an hour at least, the dogs sleeping quietly. When it was time to go my friend and I carried the stove outside and put it in the sled. The dogs didn't move.

Except for Storm.

He raised his head, opened one eye, did a perfect double take—both eyes opening wide—and sat up. He had been facing the front. Now he turned around to face the sled—so he was facing away from the direction we had to travel when we left—and watched us load the sled.

It took some time as the stove barely fit on the sled and had to be jiggled and shuffled around to get it down between the side rails.

Through it all Storm sat and watched us, his face a study in interest. He did not get up, but sat on his back end and when I was done and ready to go I hooked all the dogs back in harness—which involved hooking the tugs to the rear ties on their harnesses. The dogs knew this meant we were going to head home so they got up and started slamming against the tugs, trying to get the sled to move.

All of them, that is, but Storm.

Storm sat backward, the tug hooked up but hanging down. The other dogs were screaming to run, but Storm sat and stared at the stove.

Not at me, not at the sled, but at the stove itself. Then he raised his lips, bared his teeth, and growled at the stove.

When he was finished growling he snorted twice, stood, turned away from the stove, and started to pull. But each time we stopped at the tops of the hills to let the dogs catch their breath after pulling the sled and stove up the steep incline, Storm turned and growled at the stove.

The enemy.

The weight on the sled.

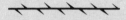

I do not know how many miles Storm and I ran together. Eight, ten, perhaps twelve thousand miles. He was one of the first dogs and taught me the most and as we worked together he came to know me better than perhaps even my own family. He could look once at my shoulders and tell how I was feeling, tell how far we were to run, how fast we had to run—knew it all.

When I started to run long, moved from running a work team, a trapline team, to training for the Iditarod, Storm took it in stride, changed the pace down to the long trot, matched what was needed, and settled in for the long haul.

He did get bored, however, and one day while we were running a long run he started doing a thing that would stay with him—with us—until the end. We had gone forty or fifty miles on a calm, even day with no bad wind. The temperature was a perfect ten below zero. The sun was bright, everything was moving well, and the dogs had settled into the rhythm that could take them a hundred or a thousand miles.

And Storm got bored.

At a curve in the trail a small branch came out over the

path we were running and as Storm passed beneath the limb he jumped up and grabbed it, broke a short piece off—about a foot long—and kept it in his mouth.

All day.

And into the night. He ran, carrying the stick like a toy, and when we stopped to feed or rest he would put the stick down, eat, then pick it up again. He would put the stick down carefully in front of him, or across his paws, and sleep, and when he awakened he would pick up the stick and it soon became a thing between us, the stick.

He would show it to me, making a contact, a connection between us, each time we stopped. I would pet him on top of the head and take the stick from him—he would emit a low, gentle growl when I took the stick. I'd "examine" it closely, nod and seem to approve of it, and hand it back to him.

Each day we ran he would pick a different stick. And each time I would have to approve of it, and after a time, after weeks and months, I realized that he was using the sticks as a way to communicate with me, to tell me that everything was all right, that I was doing the right thing.

Once when I pushed them too hard during a pre-Iditarod race—when I thought it was important to compete and win (a feeling that didn't last long)—I walked up to Storm and as I came close to him he pointedly dropped the stick. I picked it up and held it out but he wouldn't take it. He turned his face away. I put the stick against his lips and tried to make him take it, but he let it fall to the ground. When I realized what he was doing, I stopped and fed and rested the team, sat on the sled and thought about what I was doing wrong. After four hours or so of sitting—watching other teams pass me—I fed them another snack, got ready to go, and was gratified to see Storm pick up the stick. From that time forward I looked for the stick always, knew when I saw it out to the sides of his head that I was doing the right thing. And it was always there.

Through storms and cold weather, on the long runs, the long, long runs where there isn't an end to it, where only the sled and the winter around the sled and the wind are there, Storm had the stick to tell me it was right, all things were right.

And it came to Storm to grow old. Eight, nine, then ten years and he slowed. He trained many pups and, finally, he retired and stopped pulling. We tried to make him a pet and move him into the house, as we often do when dogs retire, but he didn't want that, didn't want to leave the kennel. He rattled around in the house and kept trying to walk out through the windows and glass doors, so we let him outside and kept his food dish full and left him untied.

For a year Storm was the old man in the kennel. He sat in the sun and played with the pups and watched the team leave and come back and always he had a stick. He would hold the stick when I came out to the kennel to harness and when I returned from a run.

And another year passed and he grew blind and his thinking changed so that he was not always aware but still he was happy. He sat by his house and when he heard my steps coming, he would hold his stick out for me. Sometimes I

77

would go to his house and sit next to it in the sun and he would lay his head in my lap with the stick in his mouth and I would think of things I had forgotten about; young things and old things, long runs and short runs, puppies and cold and wind, northern lights and firelight against snow, the creaking sound of an old-fashioned lashed sled moving beneath me, and the joy, the raw-cold joy of going again and again inside the diamond that is northern winter, and all with Storm.

And there came a time when it was supposed to end. Storm failed and began to wander aimlessly through the kennel, bouncing off other dogs' houses, and I knew it would not be long until he faced east as so many of them did when they died. I wanted to leave him loose for that, so he could find the right place.

But we had some new dogs and some of them were aggressive and insecure and wanted to fight all the time. They would even almost fight old Storm when he came too close to their circles, though it was very rare for young dogs to attack older, more respected ones. I did not want Storm to end that way, in violence, so when I went on a trip one fall day I left Storm tied to his chain.

It was a temporary thing, just until I got back, but while I was gone it came on Storm to end and in the final time of his life he somehow got the chain wrapped around his doghouse so he could not face east, could not do it properly.

I saw where he had struggled and torn at the ground with his old claws to get around, to face east as so many animals do if there is time in the end but he could not. He could not tear the chain out of the ground, could not wear it around, could not move the house, could not face the east and end it right.

And it was my fault. I should have known that this was the day he would end, should have felt that he was going to die. I should have known to let him loose, even if there was a risk of a fight. After all, it would be natural for him to fight—they love to fight.

But I did not.

It was my fault and when death came and Storm could not face east he knew that I would be upset. Storm knew I would feel bad, and he did the only thing he could do.

When I came back the next day I went to the kennel and there was silence until I came close and then the dogs went into the death song, which sounds much like the rain song, and I knew then Storm was gone. Knew before I saw him, knew before I even arrived at the kennel. It is a low song, that stays low and does not go into the keening whine that means excitement and I felt all the sadness that comes with the end of a life and went to take his body from the kennel and bury him.

I found him next to his house. He had jammed into the side, trying to get around to the east. The earth was torn beneath him, the chain held his head north.

But he didn't blame me.

I will always blame myself, but Storm did not blame me.

His last act, his last thought, was for me. Storm lay dead and in his mouth was a stick, the stick.

Our stick.

· 8 ·

THE wind seemed to scream as we cut through the night. It had been a cold week—fifty-three below one night, forty-five below the next two, and never rising above twenty below with wild wind out of the northwest the whole time.

Somehow, we had gotten caught out in the worst part of the weather. The true cold had found us eighty miles out. I was not dressed for deep cold and I worried about the dogs. Two of them had frostbitten ears. As I treated them with ointment I decided to hole up until the weather eased a bit—I thought overnight.

I rigged a snow shelter and made a lean-to with a tarp and dug snow caves for the dogs and we holed up to wait until the worst of the cold had passed. We had some dog food and about twenty pounds of fat for the dogs and I had one lovely, lovely can of Chef Boyardee ravioli.

We hunkered in for the duration.

I lasted a day looking at the ravioli, drinking hot "tea" (I had one tea bag which I used over and over). Hunger set in and I used two small pieces of the dogs' fat and mixed it with half the ravioli for a stew.

It tasted wonderful and I ate it, waited another half a day and ate the rest, and it wasn't so bad.

The wind roared but the dogs were covered—I fed them twice and re-covered them—and it could have gone on. I had plenty of wood for fire and the wind was away from me.

But on the morning of the third day I became violently ill. I thought it might be the flu, when I could still think, or food poisoning from the pieces of fat. Then it didn't matter.

I went into a high fever and delirium. I began to hallucinate and while hallucinating somebody arrived (a man I did not know) and he "helped" me harness my team.

The wind was still bad and the dogs did not want to leave their warm snow caves but my helper gave a hand. He was a short man, thick through the middle with curved, sloping, strong shoulders and a great confidence and knowledge of dogs. He shook the dogs out of the snow and made them stand in the wind and twice looked at me and smiled. His face was flat and oval and his eyes were gentle. He signaled me to go, motioning with his hands to move the team, to get the dogs to run. I caught the sled as it went by and I think I tried to wave at him as we left in the dark.

I know looking back on it that it was a hallucination. I can sit and think of it and know that, but it was still real.

I don't remember that whole run. It was a series of nightmares, of dreams mixed with reality, of scenes and movements and pictures.

I tried to ride on the back of the sled but I was too sick and kept falling. Fumbling in the dark and cold and wind, I used some rope to tie myself to the sled and still fell many, many times. Each time the dogs would stop and let me get back on the sled. When it was finally too much and I couldn't stand, I crawled into the sled and wrapped myself in my sleeping bag—which the man had helped me pack—and let the dogs have me.

I could not sleep, but kept going in and out of consciousness. Once when I felt that we were stopped I looked up, out of the bag, and the man—the same man who had helped me leave the clearing, the Eskimo man—was pulling my lead dog out of a drift that had blown in over the trail. Again, when the dogs were straightened out and moving he waved to me as the sled passed close to him. I waved back and reached for him but could not touch him as the sled moved rapidly away.

Through that long night we ran. It was very hard going for the dogs, fighting the wind and the snow, and I couldn't help them, lying half dead in the sled. Many times they were stopped, hung up in deep snow or trying to fight their way through large drifts, and each time I raised in the sled and saw the man in the parka with the wolf-fur trim around the hood grab the leader by the back of the harness and help him through the bad part.

Once I became sick and leaned over the side of the sled and was violently ill and the dogs turned and came back to eat it, which made me sicker. They were an awful mess, tangled and piled on each other and fighting over the vomit. I was so weak that I could not stand. One of them was a large dog named—of all things—Clarence and he loved to fight. Of course many of them do, but Clarence was so large and strong that when he fought he could do serious damage and he jumped on another dog named Yogi and started to kill him. He had Yogi by the throat and I could do nothing.

And the man was there again. The man with no name was there and he smiled peacefully and quietly and untangled the dogs with his gentle competence and pulled them out straight and got them going again, then stood back as we went by and I tried once more to touch him but could not.

And again.

We came to a place in the dark wind where the trail was gone. There had been a trail there when we went out but a logging crew had gone through with a skidder and the blade had taken the trail down to bare ice. It was a steep downhill grade and I was not on the back of the sled where I could use the brakes. The sled began to creep up on the dogs and as it did, it lost steering and turned sideways and rolled over. I was dumped into the side of a pine tree with gear and dog food, and the dogs balled up again in a horrible pile at the bottom of the hill. I couldn't see them well in the dark and tried to crawl to them but everything was blurred and the man came again, the friend.

He lined the dogs out and put the gear back in the sled and set the snowhook so they couldn't run until he'd helped me back into the sled. Then he pulled the hook and put it into the sled and I waved once more and thanked him. He ignored me and called to the dogs with a short sound, a word that sounded like an explosion in his mouth: "Httcha!"

And the dogs took off again, running for him, and I went into the sleep-unconsciousness once more.

Somewhere there was a lake with bad ice and the front end of the team picked their way across it and somewhere we ran down a creek bed on the ice and there was open water and the dogs worked around it. I saw these things as if in a dream. We bounced off many trees and I hit my head several times and was sick again—though the dogs kept going this time—and finally I remembered and saw nothing until I felt the sled was stopped, stopped dead. I opened my eyes and saw that we were in the kennel and the dogs were rolling and scratching at their harnesses, waiting to be let out so they could shake their legs and sleep in their houses. My wife came out and helped me—I was staggering and not being effective at putting them away—and I tried to tell her about the man, my new friend, but it came out all confused. So I stopped and thought I would tell her later but I didn't, somehow, and did not speak of him or see the man, my new friend, again for a long time.

Until I had trained in Minnesota and gone north into Alaska to run in the Iditarod and hit a place called the Burn.

It is, of course, madness—a kind of channeled, focused madness.

The Iditarod.

The idea is that the musher will take a team and go from downtown Anchorage to downtown Nome, some eleven hundred plus miles across the Alaskan wilderness, over mountain ranges, up the Yukon River, out to the coast of the Bering Sea, and up along the coast and across parts of the sea ice to Nome.

That is the idea.

And on the face of it, with the world the way it is now, with planes and computers and cars with brains and comfort-controlled environments and every single whim catered to by technology—with all of that, all that we have become—it doesn't somehow seem possible to do something so basic and elemental. It is such a massive undertaking, such a logistical complication to train a team and take them up to Alaska and run the race. The only way to do it is to break it down to simple, small units of time.

The first run took seventeen days and fourteen hours and it can be remembered best in days.

THE RACE

· DAY 1 ·

OUT of Anchorage. Just madness. There is no sleep the night before, two nights before, trying to get everything ready, no sleep or rest. The food is all shipped to twenty checkpoints across the state, the dogs are trucked into downtown Anchorage to the staging area on Fourth Street where there is—ridiculously—no snow and they must bring it in. Because the snow is shallow the sleds cut through to bare asphalt, so there is no steering, no real control. The dogs are insane to run. We pull number thirty-two—about the middle of a seventy-team race—and the dogs get to stand and watch thirty-one teams go out ahead of them. Out and down four blocks to turn sharp right and head out of the downtown section. Thirty-one teams to watch and then they take us into the chutes and the dogs know it is our time. They lunge and tear and pull and scream until they count us down and we are released. Some new dogs, some old. Cookie is there, and Storm and Fonzie and Columbia and Yogi from the work team, and new dogs that I almost don't know yet.

Forward. They blow out of the chutes so hard that my arms are jerked nearly out of the sockets and I cannot believe they are the same fifteen dogs I have trained, have run so many times before. I am as nothing on the rear of the sled, nothing. We pound the four blocks in a heartbeat. I know we cannot make the turn and we don't. The dogs sweep around, there is a moment when there seems to be control and then I roll, over and over, but hang onto the sled somehow and slide out of downtown Anchorage on my face, dragging on the back of the sled like garbage.

Only the sled and the dogs on the team matter, so little is known of other teams until much later, after the first three days. Some do not make it out of Anchorage. One musher breaks an arm, another a shoulder—three, five blocks out and they must scratch.

And that is the worst.

To scratch. Before the race it is spoken of as a disease. I am a leper, I will scratch—it is the same. Many will, but nobody wants to. Everyone wants to finish.

I regain control of the team, get back upright on the runners, and somehow get out of Anchorage. It is still not real, a dream. Finally, out of the chutes, really, really starting to run the Iditarod. The dream. The run. The Run.

And it's all phony. The show start in Anchorage is done for television, and to give Anchorage publicity. Teams can't truly go from Anchorage to Nome because the freeway system coming into Anchorage blocks the trail. The whole first start, the madness of it, the chutes, all of it has to be done over. Thirty miles out of town is the suburb of Eagle River where the dogs are put in trucks and taken eleven miles to Settler's Bay where the true race starts.

More chutes. More slamming and screaming and waiting for the front teams to leave and again, madness. The dogs blow out of the starting chutes and scramble for speed and this time it is into the bush, directly into the wilderness, but this sham start and restart has taken all day, and so the race truly starts at the end of the day.

Close to dark.

With the darkness comes chaos. The teams will not rest this first night—they are too excited and must be allowed to run until they settle in—so the darkness brings a particular insanity of passing teams and tangles and moose.

Moose.

My team stops dead in the dark and I go up to investigate the reason and find my leader (some run two leaders but I favor one), a sweet but simple dog named Wilson. I am trying to get him to lead so I can save Cookie for later, and I find him with his head between the back legs of a moose, frozen with terror. The moose, a large cow, turns to look at me when my headlight comes across her, then turns away. I do not have a gun, do not know what to do.

"What the hell are you waiting for?" a voice demands suddenly from the rear as another team runs up on mine in the dark. "Why are you stopped?"

"There's a moose," I yell back lamely.

"Well, kick it in the butt and get moving or get out of the way. . . ."

I try, kicking the moose in the left flank, and to my amazement she jumps and moves slowly off the trail so we can pass. (Later in the race I will try this again and the second moose will jump on me instead of off the trail, making my life very interesting for about five seconds.)

And on. In the confusion, my leader gets lost and takes a wrong turn while I am looking down into the sled bag and we go forty, fifty miles in the wrong direction, up into some canyons where the trail gets narrower and narrower until it finally just stops.

I go up to the front of the team in the darkness and drag them around, realizing we are lost. My clothes have been ripped on tree limbs and my face is bleeding from cuts, and when I look back down the side of the mountain we have just climbed I see twenty-seven head lamps bobbing up the trail. Twenty-seven teams have taken our smell as the valid trail and are following us. Twenty-seven teams must be met head on in the narrow brush and passed and told to turn around.

It is a nightmare. The whole crazy night turning teams, stopping fights, yelling at dogs, and wading in armpit-deep snow until, finally, we are all back on the right trail, and at last just before dawn I can stand it no longer—three nights now without sleep—and I pull the team off on a narrow turnoff and sit on the sled to rest. To doze.

I was not there ten minutes, lying back with my eyes

closed, when I heard footsteps on the snow. An older man who is famous stood next to me in the darkness and smiled down and said:

"Would you like a chocolate chip cookie?"

Wonderfully, incredibly, miraculously he has somehow gotten two chocolate chip cookies through that mad night without breaking them. He handed me one and I sat up and poured tea from my thermos into my cup and his and we drank the tea and dunked the cookies and did not talk but just sat. I looked at my watch and found it was exactly twenty-four hours since we were in the staging area in downtown Anchorage waiting to get in the starting chute.

It is the end of the first day.

· DAY 2 ·

AT dawn we break into the open from thick, dark forest and are treated to a spectacular sight. The sun coming over our right rear lights up the entire Alaska Range across our front. There are no clouds and the mountains, McKinley on the right, tower over us in dazzling white enormity, filling the sky while the sun warms our backs and the dogs settle into running.

The madness of the night is gone. The front-end teams, the faster runners, have moved on and we (the dogs and I) are left to get down to the business of running better than a thousand miles.

It is a strange thing to do.

The dogs are magnificent. They are the true athletes of the Iditarod. The dogs continually cause wonder with their endurance, joy, and intelligence. But they have tremendous needs. They must be fed a snack every hour or so, and three

94

or more hot meals a day. Their shoulders must be rubbed every hour and they must be allowed to shake the lactic acid buildup out of their joints each hour.

And their feet . . .

God, their feet. I am being pulled by fifteen dogs and that makes sixty feet to be taken care of; to be watched and rubbed with ointment and covered with booties if need be.

So much time will be spent on my knees that I have sewn half-inch foam pads into my pants at the knees to keep my legs from freezing when I kneel in the snow.

And in this business of running, this whole business of getting started and settling down to taking care of the dogs, in the tension and speed of the race I do not notice when we start climbing; beginning the long run up into the mountains. We move through the day up some frozen rivers and across some frozen lakes and when it gets dark again we come into the first of twenty checkpoints.

Noise and pandemonium. Dog teams coming and going, judges and spectators all around. Small planes landing on the ice and taking off. The dogs cannot rest because of the noise. I get my sacks of food and we head up the river a bit to be alone, but still they do not rest. They sit and watch other teams coming and going, watch the planes taking off over us.

Even in the dark, in the willows at the side of the river, it is crowded. A man with a team wanders in circles out in front of me, the dogs running around and around on the ice, jumping from one snowmobile trail to the next and circling back, confused by all the trails in the darkness.

Everybody is confused.

When it is clear the dogs will not rest, I hook up their tugs and we start off again. We luckily find the right trail and as we leave the checkpoint the man whose team was wandering follows us out.

That night passes again in confusion. Teams pass us, we pass other teams. I stop to rest the dogs again but they still will not sleep—won't, indeed, for two more nights—so I let them run. The snow is unbelievably deep. When I stop them and run up alongside the team at one point to work on their feet I mistakenly step off the trail and go in up to my armpits. I have to crawl out by grabbing at the dogs and using them for an anchor.

And my brain fries that second night.

Sleep deprivation catches me and I start hallucinating. We have been warned about that in briefings, along with frostbite, wind, whiteouts, wind, intense cold, and finally, wind. But nothing can prepare you for your first hallucinations in the race because they are not dreams, not something from sleep or delirium; the intensity of the race, the focused drive of it makes for a kind of exhaustion in the musher not found in training. The hallucinations seem to roar at you. They come while you are awake, come with your eyes open, and are completely real.

There is a small bit of snow that spurts up from each dog's foot as they run, a little white jet, and that turns in my mind to flame. I see my dogs all running in flame, their feet and lower legs on fire. Terrified, I set the snowhook and run up to put the fire out, lean down to pat the flames out and of course they disappear, are not there.

But the vision comes again and again until at last I some-how reconcile myself by thinking it is all right because the flames do not hurt the dogs. I am amazed that they can run in liquid fire and not feel pain or get injured.

The hallucinations do not go away. Indeed, they get more complicated. Often I nearly get lost by going up rivers that aren't there, following lights that do not exist.

At one point I have a man sitting on my sled. He is wearing a trench coat and a pair of horn-rimmed glasses and is holding a manila folder full of official-looking papers. As I watch he turns to look up at me—he is very distinct and I can see the wrinkles in the fabric of his coat, my own reflection in his glasses—he turns to look at me and begins to speak in a low voice about federal educational grants.

He is the most boring human being I have ever met—as dull as thick mud—and he goes on and on until at last I yell at him to shut up.

The dogs stop and look back at me and of course I am alone.

It is only in the night when the hallucinations are bad—between about eleven and four in the morning—and I will not learn how to truly control them for another day and a half.

The night drags on forever as the dogs keep trotting and I reel in and out of half-sleep on the back of the sled, but at long last it is dawn. There is cold now at dawn, deep cold. It is perhaps fifty below. And I come alongside a musher whose teeth are chattering—a bad sign—while he tries to get a fire going.

"Cold," he says, the word a benediction.

I nod from the closed tunnel of my parka hood and pull my team over to rest. They are at last ready to stop.

It is the end of day two.

· DAY 3 ·

WE must cross the Alaska Range.

Somebody before the race kept saying it was the highest mountain range in North America—which is true—and it takes all of this day climbing and another one climbing still more to get up into the peaks.

We pass through three more checkpoints, two of them villages with children running out to watch the teams come through. They are intensely curious and study each thing I do as I feed and take care of the dogs. One checkpoint is a trapper's cabin where we may stop but are not allowed inside the cabin.

My team is very slow, much slower than most other teams and I realize on this day that I will be very lucky to finish the race, let alone do well. Finishing is all I originally wanted, but the hot worm is always there—the thought that maybe your dogs are special and will prove themselves better than Rick's or Susan's or any of the other front-end runners. It is a futile dream, a strange thought to have, but it is there nonetheless.

Until this third day.

The mountains, the climbing and climbing, have a way of establishing reality. As the team climbs into the peaks above timberline and comes out at the Rainy Pass checkpoint where there are thirty or so other teams stopping to feed and rest, I have entered into a state of almost idiotic bliss.

I am tired beyond belief. Beyond how it was in the army. Beyond anything I have known, I am tired. But the team is moving and seems healthy and everybody is eating and drinking and the scenery is so beautiful that it doesn't matter how far we're behind.

I am steeped in beauty. It is like going back ten, twelve thousand years, running over these mountains with a dog team. Like becoming a true human—a human before we became cluttered by civilization. Like going inside and becoming a cave painting.

We end the third day in the Rainy Pass checkpoint, resting. I sit on the sled and stare at the dogs while they sleep. My eyes close and when they open again—it seems a moment—four hours have passed.

Yogi is up, jerking around, wanting to fight, and I realize it is time to go.

· DAY 4 ·

OVER Rainy Pass and down through the gorge.

Everybody warned the rookies about the gorge, also known as "The Gut" and "The Chute."

It is a twenty-mile downhill run through a river gorge studded with boulders and you run on an ice ledge steeply down, weaving in and out of the boulders for the whole distance. The other mushers tell the rookies that it is easy to get in trouble in the gorge.

And it is.

In a moment of sheer stupidity, worried that I will lose my team, I tie my left arm to the sled. Seconds later I am knocked off the sled and as the dogs careen down through the gorge they loop out and around a boulder but the sled does not make it cleanly and hits the boulder and I am knocked off the runners and I cannot get up. I bounce, bang off boulders, swing back and forth like a piece of meat. I seem to do most of the gorge run on my back, whamming boulders with the top of my head.

Through a miracle or two my stupidity in tying myself to the sled does not kill me. A musher stopped at the end of the gorge fixing his broken sled grabs my team and pulls them to a stop as they pile into a small side ravine or I think it would have been worse.

Tattered, bleeding, ragged, and stunned I come out the end of the gorge to crash in the next checkpoint and spend the day recovering.

It is the end of day four.

· DAY 5 ·

AT Rhone River I take my twenty-four hour mandatory layover.

I sleep on the ground with the dogs near a small cabin that is the checkpoint and when I awaken it is about mid-morning—I have about ten hours before I am due to leave—and I find that we are on a small island in a frozen river. It is the most beautiful spot I have ever seen.

The island is surrounded by mountains that shoot up to the sky. The peaks tower over the cabin, making it like a jewel in a giant, magnificent setting. I go to the back side of the island for water for the dogs and stand level with the bottom edge of a mountain that seems to go up forever, have to turn my head back and up to see the peak covered with snow.

It is like a cathedral. My head stops aching and the sharp

pain in my ribs goes down as I sit on a log and drink tea and let the beauty work into me for that whole day.

Rumors tear through the checkpoint like wildfire. One man is missing and feared dead. Two men are missing and feared dead. One woman was attacked by a moose and killed. Somebody was dragged to death coming down Rainy Pass in the gorge. None of the rumors are true, but they fly back and forth through the resting teams at the checkpoint, and I would be more worried by them except that I have been in the army and it has the same kind of rumor engine.

Late afternoon comes and the checker tells me I can go.

The dogs fairly hum with energy, having slept and rested for a full twenty-four hours. I stand on the sled and reach to release the snowhook but before I can they lunge and break the rope and I am gone out of the checkpoint, looking back at the snowhook as I leave.

It is the end of day five.

· DAY 6 ·

IN the dark we roar wildly through some trees that come so close to the trail the sled seems hardly to fit through. Twice I am knocked off the sled and scramble back on. Then we climb up a frozen riverbed and waterfall in the dark—the dogs jump up from boulder to boulder and I hang beneath the sled at one point with my feet out in open space—and suddenly we come out in the Burn.

We were warned about the Burn. It is a ninety-mile-wide stretch of broken country where a forest fire took everything out. For some reason there is often not very much snow in the Burn and this year is no exception. Just as it gets dark I look out across a vast expanse of rocks and dirt and dead grass and burned trees fallen across one another and no snow—not a flake—as far as I can see.

The dogs are still fresh, having slept a full day, and they don't care that there is no snow for the sled runners—it's all the same to them—and I have to run them. Inside half a mile I'm in trouble.

The dogs run beneath a burned tree and the sled jams. I cannot back them up so I take a small bow saw and cut through the tree, which allows the sled to escape. I barely grab on as it explodes forward.

To the next tree.

And the sled jams and I cut through the tree again; all through the dark night we slam from tree to tree with me dragging on my face half the time, bouncing off rocks and dirt while the dogs—resting each time I must cut a tree—stay fresh and powerful and lunging.

It is chaos.

I have not rested well and the hallucinations start about midnight and I have the same man in the trench coat on the sled for a time, talking to me about educational grants, until I tell him to shut up and leave and he becomes indignant.

I learn that night how powerful the hallucinations can be. In a rare moment when the sled is on smooth ground I come across a clearing and a dog team is stopped ahead of me.

All the dogs are asleep, spread out across the grass and one of the other mushers in the race is leaning over the empty sled with his fist raised.

"Get out of the sled or I'll kill you," he is saying and when I stop in back of him and ask him what is wrong he points down to the empty sled.

"It's this man. I've carried him over two hundred miles

and he won't help push up the hills. I'm sick of him. I'm going to leave him here in the Burn. . . ."

We talk for a bit and he relaxes and realizes he is hallucinating but as I leave I hear him say loudly again, "Get out of the sled. . . ."

And I think as we go that perhaps it is not real and I am hallucinating about a man having hallucinations and that in turn triggers the thought that perhaps all of it—the Burn, the race, the dogs, my life, all of it in the whole world is just a hallucination. My brain is running wild with this thought when the dogs stop and I look up and there is an enormous bull buffalo standing in front of my leader, smelling his head.

I stare at it for a long time. The man in the trench coat is back on my sled and the buffalo is standing there. My befuddled brain simply thinks it's another hallucination and I wait for it to disappear.

It doesn't.

I try to hush the man on the sled because I am worried he will anger the buffalo. I have never seen an angry buffalo, even in a hallucination, and do not want to start now. The buffalo seems as big as a house, but it slowly seeps into my thinking, like mud warming, that the dogs would not have stopped for my hallucination.

It is a real buffalo.

There is a herd of real buffalo in the Burn and this bull stands looking down on my leader—Wilson, who is very sweet and a wonderful dog but dumber than a walnut— smelling him.

I call the dogs up and they go around the bull and I am surprised when the man on the sled says nothing though we pass not four feet from the buffalo and could easily touch it. The buffalo does nothing to us, is very mellow.

I hear later that another musher fell asleep in the Burn next to his sled—his dogs were resting—and when he woke up the buffalo was standing over him, straddling him, smelling the breath as it came out of his nostrils.

Buffalo, he says when he tells of it—there is strangely no fear in his voice—have very bad breath.

The Burn, finally, becomes too much. I am going across a large clearing—several miles across—and it starts to snow and the wind kicks up until I cannot see the dogs, only the front end of the sled now and then, and I have no idea where the trail is supposed to be.

Wilson loses his way and begins to wander. Since there is no trail to follow he works around in a large circle to the right and heads off into the bush and I don't know anything of this until we come into a box canyon and cannot proceed any farther and I know we have lost the trail. We have run perhaps thirty or forty miles off the trail, and to compound the problem the wind and driving snow have quickly covered our tracks so we cannot easily find our way back and I cannot think, cannot begin to think. I sink down on my knees next to the sled in a kind of surrender, and when I look up, my friend is there.

The Eskimo man who helped me when I was sick is there and he takes Wilson by the back of his harness and drags the team around and I stand on the sled and we start.

I do not know where we are going but I have great confidence in the man with the curving shoulders and gentle smile and think that if we move slowly, just keep moving, he will not let me down.

Hours pass and each time I hesitate he shows up next to the team and waves me on. I keep going, against the wind and snow, until I look down and see sled tracks. They are filling fast so they must be very fresh. I call the dogs to increase speed and we run through the rest of the darkness and at dawn I see a cabin which signals the end of the Burn. I wish I could thank the man who saved me again but he is gone.

It is the end of day six.

· DAY 7 ·

IN and out of a checkpoint—a village named Nicolai. It is very crowded with snowmobiles roaring by and resting teams all around, so I don't stay. The wind stops and the sun comes out.

Everything again is steeped in beauty as I run down a river and over some large hills and we come around a corner in the brush, run up off the river and there is a bar.

In the middle of nowhere a man suddenly appears and asks me if I want a beer. I say no, I don't drink, and he gives me a soda instead. It tastes incredibly wonderful and I drink it down in one long swallow. While I am turned away he throws three more sodas in my sled.

It is a very nice thing to do except that I don't see him do it and leave the checkpoint without knowing the sodas are there. They settle down on top of my booties in the bootie sack and that night it gets forty or fifty below and the cans of soda freeze and burst. The next day it gets warm again; the sodas thaw and run into the cloth booties and refreeze in the cloth.

Later that day Wilson cuts his foot and I go to get a bootie for him and find they are frozen in soda slush. I thaw one in my armpit and put it on his foot and we start off.

Wilson smells the soda.

If it smells interesting, he thinks, it must taste good. Soon he is running on three legs sucking on his foot and that's the way I pass a team which is resting, with my leader running on three legs sucking a foot.

The musher just nods and watches Wilson run by.

We run all day on a beautiful trail, down some long, long hills into a checkpoint where a beautiful blond girl hands me a cup of hot chocolate. It is not possible for anything to taste as good as that hot chocolate tastes and I drink it slowly, trying to make it last.

I leave the checkpoint in the dark. The land has flattened into long hills like ocean swells and the wind has died down and the team runs well through the night while I stand on the back lost in hallucinations again. This time I see crowds of people cheering for me. Some of them are riding snowmobiles and some come out of cabins to wave and I can see their families inside the cabins sitting at tables and twice I have to move quickly on the sled to keep from being nudged by the snowmobiles when they come close to wave to me.

None of it real.

Dawn comes and we are in the interior of Alaska. So different, it is like another planet. No trees, only tundra and the long low hills and the jingle of the dogs' collars and the whuffing of their breath as they trot and we cover the miles, the long miles across the interior over to the Yukon River.

It is the end of day seven.

· DAY 8 ·

IT must be the same as going to the moon, crossing the interior of Alaska by dog team. After a time it seems the team isn't moving, that the country, the tundra, the endless grass and shallow snow are rolling by beneath us and we are standing still—so unchanging is the country.

Flat, gently rolling, it is stultifying. Running through the night to get to the cabin Wilson has started to do a new thing. He falls over.

When it first happened I was worried that something was wrong and ran forward to attend him. I put him on his feet and his tail wagged and he was all right and we took off.

In thirty yards he fell over again. Once more I put him on his feet and we set out.

Over he goes.

Finally I realize that the boredom is too much and he is falling asleep while running.

I pet him and sit next to him for a time but he won't sleep to rest. Only while we run. So he isn't tired, just bored, and once more we set off.

I watch him with my light and when his back starts to weave a bit I say softly, "Willy?"

And he awakens and is fine for forty or so yards. Then he does it again and I say it once more and through that long night every forty yards I say, "Willy?"

And it works. We keep moving and everybody stays happy. During the night I pass teams and they pass me. Finally, in the morning, the team stops at a small caved-in cabin. It is not a checkpoint, but a good place to rest the dogs. Inside the cabin a man I passed and who passed me later has a fire going in the stove. So I hang my clothes to dry and make tea. We are sitting and drinking when he asks me if I ran all night.

"Yeah."

"Twice somebody went past me in the dark," he said, "looking for somebody named Willy. I wonder who that was?"

I shrugged. "I have no idea . . ." This man had seen me running while Wilson sucked his foot. I thought there was no sense in making it even worse.

And that ended day eight.

· DAY 9 ·

WE pass through the ghost town of Iditarod, which is set up as a checkpoint. I pull the team up alongside the river to rest them under some overhanging willows. The dogs and I are sitting by a fire when a plane lands right next to me and a man gets out.

"Somebody told me you had big dogs," he says, looking at my team.

"I guess so. Big and slow."

"I have a female wolf in the plane and want to breed her to some big dogs. . . ."

I look at the plane more closely and sure enough, in the back seat is a wolf. She is huge—well over a hundred pounds—and has a muzzle on. I cannot believe this man has flown out here with a wolf sitting in back of him just to get her bred by my dogs.

"She's in season," he offers. "The only problem is she's killed three male dogs I've tried to breed her to. . . ."

"I'll pass," I say, and he shrugs amiably, jumps into the plane, and takes off. It is all so bizarre I think perhaps I dreamt it, but there are ski marks on the snow from the landing gear of the plane.

We leave again at night. There are some mean hills as we leave and they are dotted with gear dropped by rookies trying to get lighter. I see an extra pair of socks, some gloves, brass snaps, a Coleman stove, a good fur hat (which I try to grab but miss and don't want to stop for), several articles of undergarments. It seems a waste but I find later that people from the checkpoint will come out with snowmobiles and harvest the hills as they do each year.

Three days earlier one of my dogs had stopped eating any of the meats I had sent for the dogs—pork, lamb, beef, liver, and dry dog food. But she would eat the meat patties I had sent for myself, which had cheese and raisins and fat mixed in. So I gave her all my own food and consequently didn't have any food at the checkpoints. Other mushers had helped me some, but a major food chain had butter and a dry beverage powder at all the checkpoints as a promotional stunt. So when I left a checkpoint I'd take four or five pounds of butter with me. I was eating sticks of butter as I went across the interior to maintain energy.

As might be imagined I became truly sick of butter—don't like it much yet—and when I got to the Shageluk checkpoint I was glad to find that the children from the school had a huge pot of moose chili cooking in the council hall just for the mushers.

It tasted wonderful and I could not stop eating it. Like a wolf, I gorged—ate nineteen paper bowlfuls of chili.

I then start the run up the Yukon River and inside of four hours I thought I was going to die of gastric distress. At one point it became so bad that the team stopped and looked back at me in surprise.

End of day nine.

· DAY 10 ·

THE run up the Yukon River is horrific. A hundred and eighty miles straight north into the wind, up the middle of the great river that historically is a highway across Alaska. In the summer barges bring supplies up the river to the villages. Now snowmobiles whiz by frequently as people go from one village to the next to visit.

All the cold air in Alaska seems to settle into the Yukon Valley and in the night it hits like a hammerblow.

Forty, fifty below—and colder. Going up the middle of the river in the deep cold night is like going inside an iceberg.

I cannot stand the wind. I turn backward on the sled and hook my elbows and ride but it is still too cold. I put on all my extra clothes and it is still too cold. I feel the cold cutting through all the clothing. I go up to check the dogs but they are all right—no signs of frostbite—so we continue. There is nowhere to stop at any rate.

Just ice. Flat ice and wind. We fight north the whole day and through the night and stop to rest in the morning at dawn around in back of an island to get out of the wind.

The cursed, cutting, tearing, soul-cold wind.

I sit on the sled with my back to the wind and let the new sun warm my face and it is the end of day ten.

· DAY 11 ·

ANOTHER long day and into the night and the bone-chilling cold. This terrible night I get too cold. The cold is coming down on me like a death, and I must run to keep my body temperature up.

I run fifty paces and ride fifty and run fifty and ride fifty the whole night and the running brings my body heat back up. But I cannot get enough air through my two wool masks so I pull them down and breathe straight into my mouth. I get enough air then, but the cold raw air freezes the sides of my throat and blood vessels burst and my throat generates mucus and soon I am choking on it.

It is very hard to clear. I must stick a finger down my throat to help pull it out and when I throw it on the ice the wheel dogs turn around and eat it. This makes me throw up and they eat that as well and I spend the whole day and night running up the river hacking blood and mucus and vomiting and hallucinating.

When I approach the village that is the last checkpoint on the Yukon River I look up on some cliffs on the left side of the river and see a bunch of crosses. We have been told about the graveyard to the south of town and I feel the ghosts of all the dead in the graveyard welcoming me to the end of the river run. It is a warm feeling, a gentle calling. I nod to them and smile and turn off the river on the overland trail out to the Bering Sea.

It is the end of the river and the end of day eleven.

· DAY 12 ·

THERE is a change on this day, in the dogs and in me. We run down from the river out to the Bering Sea on a classic run. It is about zero or slightly above and there is sun and it is downhill for over ninety miles and the dogs run to my mind.

I have changed, have moved back in time, have entered an altered state, a primitive state. At one point there is a long uphill grade—over a mile—and I lope alongside the sled easily, lightly, pushing gently to help the dogs. My rhythm, my movement, is the same as the dogs. We have the same flow across the tundra and I know then we will finish.

We could run forever into the wind, across the short grass, run for all the time there has been and all the time there will be and I know it and the dogs know it.

We come out to the coast at an Eskimo village and one

of the villagers, an older man, takes me in for the night and feeds me with great gentleness and talks to me while I sit in his small house. When my eyes close and won't open he shows me a bed he has prepared for me.

As I go to sleep I see him walk by wearing only long underwear and he looks the same as the man who saved me in the Burn and earlier when I was sick. He has the same curved, strong shoulders and a quiet soft strength. When I awaken some hours later and check the dogs and get ready for the run up the coast he comes out to wish me well.

We run out of the village north with the sun coming up on our right, heading north again, the only direction, and it is the end of day twelve.

· DAY 13 ·

THERE is something about the ocean that affects me. It is open offshore, not frozen, and blue from the sky, and though it's about twenty below it is a soft cold and the dogs are full of it. They won't stop to rest, keep hitting the harnesses. One female named Blue starts shredding her harness with great glee as a joke each time I stop to feed or rest if I don't get her the food fast enough.

I am sitting in the fourth to the last checkpoint when the race ends. We still have two hundred or so miles to go, across part of the ice on Norton Sound, and it is completely over. They're having their banquets and the winner is being paid and there is cheering and I still have four days to go to finish.

And we do not care.

We run the hills easily. Letting the team do as they wish,

I simply stand on the back or push up the hills and do not care about winning or losing—only the dance counts.

The beauty is, as through the whole race, staggering. The hills which would once have put me off with their steepness are full of light and game. Clouds of ptarmigan rise like giant white snowflakes into a bright sun in front of the dogs—sometimes two, three hundred of them. And the strange arctic hares that stand on their back legs to see better are all over the place. They seem to be people, especially in the twilight as evening comes and the edges of hallucinations start. I keep thinking there are people standing in back of bushes to watch us pass.

Finally the dogs can stand it no longer and they take off from the trail, chasing one of the hares, and I get a thrilling ride down a long hill. The hare easily outdistances the dogs and they wheel back up the hill in a single, sweeping circle. They do not care that they failed to catch him.

The dogs fairly hum with energy as we slide gleefully down the final hills into the checkpoint just before we go out on the ice and it is the end of day thirteen.

FROM Shaktolik we must cross Norton Sound. Depending on who is telling you it is apparently about sixty miles of sea ice. Horror stories abound about the Sound.

Rumors.

Somebody has gone through the ice and they found her team wandering alone.

Somebody else went insane and is making big circles out on the ice but nobody wants to stop him because he will be disqualified if he is given help.

Somebody was found dead on her sled.

Somebody was torn from his sled by the wind and the dogs blew thirty miles across the ice sideways and he didn't find them for two days.

Somebody was on a large cake of ice and it broke loose and headed out to sea. They are worried that she will not be found or may drift across the Bering Sea to Russia.

Somebody froze his eyeballs because he didn't blink enough and is blind but is finishing the race anyway.

Somebody froze his nose and it will have to be amputated.

All of the rumors are virtually unfounded but they rip through the area as they did at Rainy Pass and I leave the checkpoint at dawn to head across the ice with some doubt.

It is the end of day fourteen.

· DAY 15 ·

THE ice gives us a joy run.

The wind abates, the sun comes out, the trail across is flat—frozen seawater—and the dogs are well rested. We fly. I let them lope easily in a gentle canter for close to forty miles before they come down into a trot and when we stop to rest several of the dogs actually start playing like puppies, crouching down and bouncing toward each other.

The day passes in a kind of Gidget-goes-to-Nome happiness and when darkness comes I see the lights of the checkpoint across the flat ice and the dogs do as well and they start running towards them in the same easy lope.

Distances are very deceiving out on the ice however and we still probably have thirty or so miles to go. In a while it seems as if the lights will never get closer and the dogs break down into a fast trot that carries them all the way in.

As we enter the village a small boy leaps out of the

darkness and grabs the leaders by the back of their harnesses to lead them up to his house where I will spend the checkpoint time. It is a nice gesture but the dogs pile up on themselves, get tangled and turn inward. I am terrified they will begin fighting with the boy in the middle—children and even adults have died this way—and I run up to him and grab him by the back of his jacket and hold him up away from the dogs and ask him why he grabbed my team.

He smiles and says it is because he wants a team to stay at his house so he can learn about the dogs and sleds, and I am stunned that an Eskimo boy on the Bering Sea would have to ask someone from Minnesota about dogs.

I stay in his house and his family feeds me and they treat me with the same gentle courtesy the older man showed me earlier. I try to speak of the dogs but find that I cannot speak well, can only talk in grunts and single words, and have some trouble being with people. After a time I go back out with the dogs and sleep with them on the ice. I awaken at dawn just as a team pulls in. They look good, and fresh for just coming across the ice, and I am surprised to see the musher run forward with a little rubber duck and roll on the snow with his dogs, squeezing the squeaky toy for them and playing with them. They love the game and he keeps hiding the toy from them and they try to get it away from him.

Then he puts the duck away and dresses them in doggie sweaters so they can sleep warm and I leave the checkpoint in a kind of gladness that I had seen him; a gladness that I knew dogs and they knew me and that we had come together.

And it is the end of day fifteen.

·DAYS 16 AND 17·

TWO more checkpoints.

We run along the coast, along the edge of the ice with towering cliffs going up to our right. The ocean is breaking away the ice and finally there is nothing except water in front so we angle up into the country, across a mountain—dead over the top of it—and down across another bay on ice.

Here the wind is strong and blowing straight from the rear. The ice is sheer, flat, absolutely slick, and the wind blowing from the rear makes my body act as a sail. The sled blows forward and sideways and I must ride the break to keep from running up on the dogs all across the bay.

The dogs seem to smell Nome now. They have changed and know we are near the end and when we leave the last checkpoint but one and head out onto the beach—a forty-mile-long beach ending in Nome—they seem to have new purpose in their steps. It is perhaps all in my head, but then so much else is that it doesn't matter.

We run through the day along the edge of the beach, running on the ice itself because the wind has blown all the snow off the beach sand. As dark comes I can see the lights of the finish, of Nome, twenty or more miles ahead and when I realize what they are I stop the team.

I do not want to go in and finish the race.

I do not understand why, but I do not want to go in. I actually begin to walk up and take my leader and turn the dogs around and run back, back. . . .

There is no sense to it but somehow it is because the race is something that doesn't seem like it can be done. Not really. You can talk about it and plan for it and train for it but it is not something you can do.

The Run.

Even then, when you are making The Run it doesn't seem possible and while you are in it and crossing the Alaska Range at Rainy Pass and running through the Burn and across the interior; even when you think you are alone on the planet and then know that you are alone on the planet; even as you run out to the coast and up the coast and across Norton Sound and along the icy cliffs through all the glorious northern villages with names like Kaltag and Koyuk and Shaktolik and Unalakleet and Elim; and even when you see the lights of Nome and think you will easily finish, even then it is not something you can do.

Not something that can be done. And yet you do it and

then it becomes something you don't want to end—ever. You want the race, the exaltation, the joy and beauty of it to go on and on. . . .

And so I stopped them and thought of turning around and going back into the middle of the world, the place I had found in the center of the world where it was only the dogs and only me and I hung there for a time, with my hand on the leader's back and I think I would have turned them except that I heard a yell and it was my wife.

A man in Nome had brought her out on a small road in a jeep. They had seen me coming and seen me stop and her voice broke the spell.

I got on the sled again and let them run and they followed the ice along the beach until we hit the ramp where they launch boats and we ran up that onto Front Street and down the mile of bare asphalt to the arch, the finish line.

Cookie, the leader, stopped before the arch and I had to drag her beneath it to finish—she was afraid of the crowd of people. I turned and could not keep from crying as I hugged my wife and son and then the dogs, starting from front to back, hugging each dog until two mushers took them away to put them on beds and I turned to the mayor of Nome who was there to greet me and said the one thing I never thought I would ever say.

"We'll be back to run it again."

And I knew that it was true.

GARY PAULSEN's three Newbery Honor books, *Dogsong*, *Hatchet*, and *The Winter Room*, as well as *Sentries*, *Tracker*, and *Dancing Carl*, have made him one of today's most popular writers. Living in northern Minnesota with his wife, Ruth Wright Paulsen, and their son, Jim, he has steadily pursued his great interest in dogs and dogsledding, chronicled for the first time here.